Lorenzo Sears

Principles and Methods of Literary Criticism

Lorenzo Sears

Principles and Methods of Literary Criticism

ISBN/EAN: 9783337311872

Printed in Europe, USA, Canada, Australia, Japan

Cover: Foto ©Thomas Meinert / pixelio.de

More available books at **www.hansebooks.com**

PRINCIPLES AND METHODS

OF

LITERARY CRITICISM

BY

LORENZO SEARS, LITT. D.

Professor in Brown University

Author of " The History of Oratory from the Age of Pericles to the
Present Time," "The Occasional Address: Its
Composition and Literature"

G P. PUTNAM'S SONS

NEW YORK AND LONDON
The Knickerbocker Press
1898

The Knickerbocker Press, New York

PREFACE

AN attempt to guide a class in literature in making critical estimates of their reading resulted in the following chapters. Reference was also had to the possible needs of some who intended to serve an apprenticeship in journalism, with its incidental book-reviewing; but beyond both these purposes was kept in mind the advantage of intelligent appreciation by educated readers of such literature as should appeal to mature tastes. Accordingly sundry methods and principles of criticism have been mentioned with the intention of showing that there is a choice among them, and that the best criticism promotes good literature, of which it is itself one of the highest forms.

The treatment of this subject under the conditions imposed required mainly whatever might contribute to the intelligibility and interest of a topic which to many is somewhat vague and tedious. In consequence, much that is familiar to adepts is restated and illustrated. Many things which can be taught by labour and practice only are left to those instructors. Nor has the attempt been made to say the last word in a field of discussion the boundaries of which will always recede before the advance into it of every adventurer. Therefore those methods and principles only have been noted which appear to be most needful to beginners in the study of literature and its criticism.

While no formal classification of the chapters in separate sections has been indicated beyond the table of contents, the titles will be found to be grouped, as there, under the general topics of General Features of Criticism, Common Forms, Higher Methods, Values, and The Critic.

L. S.

BROWN UNIVERSITY,
May, 1898.

CONTENTS

GENERAL FEATURES OF CRITICISM

CHAPTER I—CRITICISM IN LITERATURE

PAGE

CHAPTER II—MOTIVES IN CRITICISM

Contents

COMMON FORMS OF CRITICISM

Chapter VI—Impressionism

Chapter VII—Censoriousness

Chapter VIII—Commendation

Contents

Contents ix

CHAPTER XVIII—THE CRITIC'S RIGHTS

CHAPTER XIX—RESPONSIBILITIES OF THE CRITIC

CHAPTER XX—THE CRITIC'S AMBITIONS

" Thou heareste thy faultes told thee ; amend them, amend them."—LATIMER.

> " Long live our friends,
> Our friends the enemy."—BÉRANGER.

PRINCIPLES AND METHODS OF LITERARY CRITICISM

I

CRITICISM IN LITERATURE

" It was the custom of the mogul to be weighed once a year in the presence of his grandees ; and by his weight the physicians determined the state of his health."—SIR THOMAS ROE.

SIXTY years ago a contributor to a magazine recounted the story of a tempest-tossed mariner who, coming upon a strange coast, and seeing a man hanging in chains, hailed the spectacle with joy as a sign of a civilised country. " In like manner," the writer adds, " we may hail as a proof of the rapid advance of civilisation and refinement the increasing number of delinquent authors daily gibbeted for the edification of the public." His application of the incident indicates the sort of sentiment which prevailed threescore years ago, and it also serves as a landmark to show how far the present generation has advanced in its views of the character and value of criticism.   A reason for the more charitable judgment, it must also be confessed, is found in the corresponding improvement and progress which the critical art itself has made, no longer giving grounds for a sentiment which, two generations ago, was not far from just.   Still, all traces of this opinion have not yet disappeared, as also all causes of it are not entirely removed.   Accordingly, it may be well at the outset to admit that the practice of literary judgment is not always regarded with the favour it deserves.

The word Criticism itself is apt to convey an unpleasant impression.   The judgment of one person by another—the commonest signification of the term—is not agreeable to the one who is judged, and sometimes not to the one who judges.   For this reason, it may be, the word has come to present its offensive side first, implying censure.   Possibly the too common tone of personal remark in conversation has affected prevailing ideas of critical comment upon literature.   Add to this an occasional revival of old-time methods in such comment, and the term becomes freighted with considerable odium. Furthermore, as literature, criticism has usually been regarded as secondary in importance and value to that which, in contrast, has been called productive, creative, or original.

It is not proposed to consider the correctness of these impressions in this chapter, but simply to observe that they stand in the way of a proper definition of criticism, as, for example, "the art of judging with correct taste." Other definitions have been given, but this has the merit of brevity and simplicity. And the literary critic is one whose province it is to pass judgment upon literary productions according to certain standards, personal or accepted. How far in any single instance the requirements of such definitions are met is another matter, in which the critic himself becomes an object of criticism. *Definition.*

After determining what criticism is, its historical position in the growth of literature should be observed in order to set it in true perspective. In general it may be said that it has usually followed periods of creative composition, and although sometimes it has been contemporary with them, the literature of judgment has commonly succeeded to those of knowledge and *Critical ages follow creative.*

power. Such was the case in the period which followed the Periclean age in Hellenic domains, especially at Alexandria, and that which came after the Augustan age in the Roman Empire. In modern times a critical century in France followed the revival of the drama, giving an impulse to criticism in that country which has increased rather than diminished with the passing years. In Great Britain critical ages succeeded the productive times of the Elizabethan and Commonwealth periods, and the age of the reviewers at the beginning of the nineteenth century followed the intellectual ferment caused by the French Revolution, and was itself accompanied by a period of original production. In most of these instances it would seem that the human intellect had partially exhausted its creative powers and required a period of rest, reflection, and restoration. Thus a literature of observation, examination, and comparison has usually sprung up after seasons of original composition. Sometimes, however, it has happened that during creative seasons the critical spirit has not been wanting, and by reason of an inferior quality of original composition it has acquired a relative superiority, as well as by its own intrinsic worth.

It is not to be understood by this that the best critical writing may not have something of a creative character in it, and be as meritorious as much that is called original or productive; but, classified by its purpose, it naturally belongs to the reflective and retrospective order, turning back to contemplate what has already been written, rather than striking out into new fields to pursue independent investigations outside the conventional limits of examination and judgment. The exceptions to this conservative method will be considered later.

Criticism may be creative, but oftener contemplative.

It does not belittle the creative tendencies of the present age to affirm that it is also largely given to critical labours. In what ratio both forms of literary activity are in operation, in our own and in other lands, it is needless to attempt to determine. Joubert has been quoted as saying that " the French seem to love the arts less for themselves than for the pleasure to be had from criticising them "; and the writer adds that " criticism is tending more and more to take the place of creation, and forms the most interesting and important part of French literary production at the present day "; also that " French literature is suffering from a surfeit of criticism." The slowness of the Saxon race to follow Romance fashions in letters affords one ex-

The present a critical age.

planation of the dissimilar conditions which prevail among English-speaking peoples. Even in Germany, a nation of critics, current literature is not the principal object of criticism.

For the present, then, suffice it to say that the critical method, combined with other forms *Critical journalism.* of intellectual activity, is at work, in varying degree, the intellectual world over. History and philosophy, physical and mental science, fiction and poetry, day by day are being written up to the latest development, form, and fashion. Close upon their last achievement follows the writer who examines and pronounces sentence upon the daily and weekly product. His judicial comment is printed in newspapers, magazines, reviews, pamphlets, and books. The volume of it, compared with any other one class of literary production, is large, to say the least. It is a critic [1] whose work goes to the bookbinder who says of journalism, that it is " the grand literary phenomenon of modern times, the huge apparatus of floating literature, of which one leading object is to review literature itself "; and also, that " the review tends to usurp the position of the literature for which reviewing exists." How voluminous this comment may be, at times, is seen when an important work

[1] R. G. Moulton, *Shakespeare ana Dramatic Art.*

in science or philosophy, in art or theology, in poetry or fiction, is thrown before the public. A few prominent authors will furnish examples of the mass of criticism with which original works have been overwhelmed in the century which has witnessed a remarkable development of the Review.

As a notable instance in the field of science the name of Charles Darwin will occur to every reader.   He has by no means been the most voluminous writer of his class.   But personally and professionally he has been favoured with *The Critical Review in several departments.* at least two hundred and thirty review articles worth mentioning in Poole's *Index of Periodical Literature*, not to count newspaper notices, editorial or critical, amounting possibly to a thousand in all. Of the character of such criticism something may be inferred from titles like these: " Darwin Answered "; " His Facts and Fancies "; " Dangers of Darwinism "; " Science against Darwin "; " Triumph of Darwin "; " His Theories "; " Darwinism and Swimming, a Theory "; " Babes and Monkeys." Huxley fares in much the same way at the hands of friends and foes, but receives less attention, only ninety-four reviews being listed against his name.   To both lists, however, may be added five hundred and fourteen articles on

Evolution, in which the two conspicuous advocates of that doctrine seldom escape mention.

Nor do the lists of critical reviews lack names distinguished in uncontroversial literature. The Duke of Argyle, Gladstone, St. George Mivart, Lang, Hutton, Drummond, and others equally prominent, have not thought it beneath their dignity to contribute to critical literature in this as in other departments of thought.

In philosophy, Herbert Spencer has called out over one hundred and fifty writers in reviews, with the usual proportion in the daily and weekly journals of his time.

As for theological criticism, it is a body of literature in itself, to which every departure from the tradition of the elders adds a fresh contribution. It is the modern form of the Holy Office of Inquisition, employed largely by critics against each other, especially in Germany.

Ruskin may be taken as the target in the field of art at whom many of his own " arrows of the chase " have been returned with Parthian skill in at least one hundred and fifty-seven articles.

In fiction, George Eliot has succeeded in causing more than two hundred and forty pens to shed much ink, of divers colours, on many pages, in long articles, and at least twice as many more in shorter " opinions " and " notices of the press."

In poetry, how many out of his five hundred and twenty-seven reviewers have had their own clear and definite ideas of Browning's verse, however indistinct some of it confessedly was to the author himself ? Tennyson has not puzzled his commentators so much, but four hundred and eighty-five of them have given their interpretation of his theories, their estimate of his rank, or their predictions about his probable immortality.

In the failure of contemporary authors to furnish further material for criticism, there are always the classics to quarry once more in order to find an overlooked gem, or a fault which former delvers have failed to discover. Work on the Shakespearian deposit began almost two centuries after it was laid down, but within the last century more than fifteen hundred pens have been picking and poking in the veins, fissures, and cross-courses of this dramatic formation. About four hundred books, pamphlets, and review articles have been written to prove that its author was or was not Francis Bacon. Even Homer is not too far away to lose his hold upon modern criticism, as may be seen by the three hundred and forty-nine articles that have been published about him in the present century, together with books and treatises.

To these newspaper, magazine, and more ponderous review articles in general criticism should be added even weightier discussions in " critical essays," and books of " impressions," " appreciations," " adventures," and " examinations." These form a considerable body of literature by themselves, and one that is growing year by year with a rapidity surpassed only by the multiplication of fiction. In France, as has been noted, critical literature is outrunning other forms to such a degree that it has been remarked that " critics are already beginning to have no resource except to criticise one another."

Essays in criticism and books.

How large the volume is of what may be called the permanent literature of criticism, accumulated through the centuries, will be partially apprehended if representative names are recalled : Aristotle, Quintilian, Longinus, Dionysius, Petronius, and Horace among the ancients; among the moderns, the Italian Vida and the Dutch Erasmus; Boileau, Rapin, Bossu, Sainte-Beuve, Scherer, Diderot, Taine, Brunetière in France; Lessing, Ulrici, Herder, Schlegel, Grimm, Gervinus in

Representative critics.

Germany; Dryden, Pope, Johnson, Roscommon, Coleridge, Wilson, Jeffrey, Hazlitt, Lamb, Hallam, Macaulay, Arnold, Ruskin, Morley, Bagehot, Gosse, Pater, Dowden, Hutton, Sainstbury, Minto, Stephen in Great Britain; Whipple, Emerson, Lowell, Hudson, White, and Stedman in America. Each of these names will suggest others of greater or less importance, some of which will find their place in these chapters. Enough, however, have been mentioned to indicate the extent and value of critical literature, and its rank among other forms of composition.

Here, then, is a company of writers who gave their impressions, opinions, or guesses about the topic on which one man and another wrote, and the way they had treated their subjects. Doubtless there were, in addition, a hundred times as many readers who passed judgment on the same performance in the seclusion of their homes, aided or unaided by their family newspaper or magazine. In many cases, however, it must be said that private opinions are founded upon a more deliberate and thorough examination of a book, and a completer knowledge of the subject than some of the reviewers bring to their task. Taking all opinions together, published and unpublished, it may be emphatically asserted that this is an age of criticism as well as of creation, and, furthermore, that the critics surpass, in numbers at least, the entire company of authors in any department of letters. Accordingly, its relative position and importance as literature gives to criticism an interest of its own. Moreover, it has its own qualities and diversities, its privileges and duties, its standards and ambitions, deserving the attention of all thoughtful readers, and particularly of those who undertake the responsibility of literary judgment.

In primitive ages this proffer of one's judicial opinion about another's literary performance Antiquity of might have been regarded as offen-criticism. sively gratuitous and impertinent. It is not difficult to imagine the rhapsodist who preceded Homer resenting an elaborate critique of his epos if pronounced by some rival. He might descend to plain prose long enough to ask, " Who requested you to give a laboured estimate of my verses ? " No doubt all the assembly who were accustomed to hear epics recited had opinions about them, more or less critical, which they felt free to exchange with one another. But the man who first wrote out his criticisms to be heard or read by the rest must have been regarded as an innovator, if not an upstart. This opinion seems to have been entertained by an authority so late as Ville-main, who was inclined to consider criticism as a decided and rather singular usurpation. But he was regarding it on the unfavourable side of the too common manner of its exercise in fault-finding. If, however, it began to be discovered by the primitive audience that the critic's perception was clearer than other men's, and that his judgment was better, leading them to reconsider their views and recast their con-clusions, his usefulness would at length be conceded. Moreover, he might before long be assigned a place in the field of letters. Ac-cordingly it is a matter of history that before Aristotle's time the critic had secured a position among literary writers. The great analyst him-self justified his claim to a share of attention from his contemporaries by his opinion of their work. Besides, he gave such prominence to the art near its beginning that he has been called the Father of Criticism, and has con-tinued to be a teacher of it through seventy-five generations with more or less acceptance.

Whatever obtrusiveness there may seem to be attached to proffered judgment of literary products, it certainly has the sanction **Present** of long usage, and, at times, has had **demand.** a conspicuous share of attention from readers and writers. It is no longer intrusive, because it is in demand, and demanded so insistently that the sources of the best supply are over-taxed. Indifferent and poor work even is sometimes accepted because the good is scarce and expensive.

Furthermore, this assured position of criticism has been won in the face of much strife. **Permanence of its position and value.** Its hand has been against almost every man, with the usual reciprocal antagonism in consequence. It has jostled the private sentiments of readers, rattled the windows in the dwellings of tradition, and run over the dear children of the author's brain. What wonder that its course has bristled with long lines of hostile pens, that its respectability has been coldly regarded by the guild of letters, and its dicta received with a grain of salt by readers! Still, both readers and writers keep a weather eye upon its prophesyings, which, it must be confessed, have had more or less of a practical and commercial value. To the publisher they bring profit and loss. To the reader they often stand instead of his own literary judgment and conscience. To the writer they are a corrective, a tonic, or a stimulant. These offices constitute its value and contribute to its permanence. There is every indication that it has come to stay. The prejudice against an alien resident may not be entirely removed, but he has made sure of his citizen-ship, and secured the office of public censor, with the modicum of good-will that goes with it. After all, the critic should not be feared or hated, for, as one has remarked in the case of pictorial art: '' he is no more than the student observer, who deals with analysis and the determination of the validity of standards; . . . and the artist himself will do better work in so far as he becomes his own most serious critic.'' [1] Such a power in the republic of letters has, however, great opportunities of suggesting to others what they ought and ought not to do. It will of course be duly grateful for any slight return of such service.

[1] H. R. Marshall, *Æsthetic Principles*, p. 187.

II

MOTIVES IN CRITICISM

"I mistrust the judgment of every man in a case in which his own wishes are concerned."—THE DUKE OF WELLINGTON.

A LITERARY habit of such wide prevalence as criticism should have causes sufficient to account for its existence and ceaseless activity. It might be explained on the ground of a proverbial generosity on the part of most people to give their opinions gratuitously about all matters within the range of their knowledge, and sometimes outside of it. This is to be expected in ordinary social converse where words are cheap and seeming ignorance embarrassing. But opinions worth printing, and, when printed, reflecting credit or discredit upon the writer or publisher, must have, or ought to have, a justifying motive and a substantial reason for their publication.

Chief among primary motives is, no doubt, the wage-earning necessity; but in order to

16

this there must be a demand for critical writing and a commercial value in it. Aside, however, from pecuniary interest in his occupation, what are some of the less material influences underlying the work of the literary critic ? An honest one might reply that the main motive beneath all his efforts is to give just and fair estimates of contemporary literature; that it is his business to set a value-mark upon whatever comes under his professional observation; that he is to do this in order that so much of the reading public as he reaches may have its attention directed to what is good, and be saved the expense and annoyance of discovering for itself what is poor, worthless, and bad. Beyond these considerations there naturally will be others of a personal character, such as a laudable ambition to do creditable work, thus earning the reputation of eminence as an authority in a somewhat difficult department; or, again, to elevate critical composition to the level of creative; or, once more, to appeal to that judicial sense which almost all readers possess, but which few are able to formulate in clear and exact expression. Such are some of the more obvious motives which underlie the labours of a majority of the best critics at the present time. Now and then one may have still higher and broader

aims of elevating the literature which he criticises, with benevolent purposes toward the
guild of authors; but for this charitable undertaking he will need to be assured of uncommon
gifts and wide personal influence. To this
may be added the pursuit of critical studies
and the practice of critical writing for the love
of it by cultivated minds, particularly when
endowed with the critical faculty—as rare a
gift at its best as the creative. Such will ask
in their pursuit of higher critical studies, What
is the secret of the charm which a writer exercises over the mind, and by what standards is
he to be estimated?

The first-mentioned purposes, however, are
the most common, constituting the ordinary
stock of working motives that inspire a large
part of critical writing in a discriminating age.
As motives they are doubtless as worthy and
effective as those which impel persons to write
in other departments of literature.

That there are lower motives which at times
give a tone and bias to criticism is too apparent
Unworthy to be denied. It would be ungra-
motives. cious to mention them in connection
with the higher, did they not cast reproach
upon the entire art and its artisans. The history of criticism furnishes many examples in
which the influence of its organs has been given

to this or that literary theory or political creed, and judgments that did not square with these hard-and-fast notions were ruled out. The reviews and quarterlies in Great Britain in the first half of the present century are full of illustrative material in this direction. Fortunately their respective proclivities are so well known that much of the intended harm is neutralised. In our own country, where the bias of every publication is not so well understood, or is not consistently unchanging from year to year, much injury may be done through the supposition that criticism is entirely above motives of interest, or free from bonds to a creed and a theory, in politics and letters, not to mention certain other forms of bondage of a commercial nature.

Still lower in the scale are the private and professional grudges which have given a sharp acidity to critical performances in former times. In the heroic age of criticism, doughty braves did not hesitate to proclaim their intention to write a man down because they hated him. The methods they employed were, for effectiveness, such as might have been envied by Dick Turpin of Hounslow Heath. It is to be feared that the perusal of their exploits has sometimes affected critical youth in a later generation, as the reading of cowboy literature has frequently stirred bloodthirsty propensities in callow striplings.

Any enumeration of ordinary motives would be incomplete if it should not include an impelling force which deserves the emphasis of final mention, namely, the faculty and habit of Comparison. The faculty of Comparison. Its relative importance among other intellectual powers will add something to the value of an art in which it is so prominent a factor. The pre-eminent place which is assigned to this elementary process may be seen in the treatment of it by writers who have made the human intellect a special study. As representing distinguished attainments and sound conclusions in this direction, as well as embodying the best thought of former times, the views may be cited of two eminent metaphysicians, whose works are recognised as of the highest authority in mental science, Sir William Hamilton and President Porter. Of Comparison, the former says: " I will show that this faculty is at work in every, the simplest, act of mind; that its every operation is only an evolution of the same elementary process; that our simple, complex, abstract, and generalised notions are all so many products of Comparison; that Judgment is identical with Comparison." Beginning with the most elementary act of comparison—the discrimination of existence from non-existence, and the ego from non-ego, myself from everything around me and beyond—he goes on to elaborate the workings of this faculty of perceiving relations between things like and unlike far beyond what can even be outlined here. Let it be enough to repeat that he makes it a basal and " original operation of the mind, a condition of every energy of thought." [1] Of it the second author says: " The mind cannot think without judging. To think is to judge. Even in providing itself materials for acts of judgment the mind must judge." [2] If this be true of the ordinary acts of the mind and its processes in other forms of composition, it is pre-eminently true in judicial criticism. For judgment in its primary idea of comparison is contained in the Greek original from which the words " critic " and " criticism " are derived almost without the change of a letter. If it be taken in its most radical signification, it is a separation and putting asunder in order to distinguish between the things parted one from the other, and then compared the one with the other,—analysis and classification in order to comparison and

---

[1] *Metaphysics*, Lectures XX. and XXXV.

[2] *The Human Intellect*, chap. v. See also Ladd's *Psychology*, p. 304 ; Baldwin's, p. 283 ; Stout, vol. i., chap. v.

pronouncing of judgment. Thus the critic is the judge and the decider, a meaning attached to his title so long ago as when he sat in judgment upon the poetic contests at Athens.

If it should seem that this principle of Comparison is a quality of criticism rather than a motive, let it be said that it is both; but it is likewise as much the one as the other. If anything, the motive is the stronger; for to compare and to judge is an unconscious tendency and habit of the mind, as uncontrollable as thinking itself. Of other motives the person is conscious, as when he has wages or reputation in mind as he labours; but he says a thing is like or unlike something else, good or bad, instantaneously. In idiomatic phrase he is "struck" with the likeness and the impression, pleasant or unpleasant, before he has time to think about it at all. If, therefore, a motive is something which determines choice, sometimes slowly and sometimes instantly, the instinctive and prompt impulse to compare and pronounce judgment must be reckoned among the most effective motives, or as something stronger. The fact that its decisions are often and deservedly termed "snap judgments" is another testimony to its involuntary action as an original and primary faculty of the mind. All the more and on this account it cannot be left out of the list of forces which are to be reckoned with in considering what criticism is and what it ought to be.

Such are some of the prime movers in the practice of the critical art. They are mixed in character, but so are the incentives to any occupation in this busy world. Elevation of motives. Nevertheless, the critic has a mission always to elevate his profession, if he believes in a law of progression and improvement. Accordingly he will sometimes ask in what respects the motives, which appear to control or inspire criticism in many places, can be amended in the future as they have already been in the past.

An answer to this question involves another in regard to the ideal object and purpose of judicial criticism. This may be said to be a determination to declare what is good or bad, as tested by the The ideal purpose of criticism. highest prevailing standards in the department of literature of which the product under consideration is an example. A prior process of induction will of course be needful in order to place the given example in its proper class. It should be determined exactly where it belongs and to what laws it should be obedient, or whether it is distinct enough from all previous forms to be a law unto itself. Once classified, however, it has become an object of comparison with other members of its class, and especially with the best. Just here Matthew Arnold's famous definition of the function of criticism will be suggested to the reader: " To know the best that is known and thought in the world, and, by in turn making this known, to create a current of true and fresh ideas."

In this synoptical statement of the office of an ideal criticism are contained the particulars of knowledge, of judgment, and of statement, in an elementary form.

Like all general principles, they are most comprehensive, inclusive, and suggestive. Fairly developed, they will be found to cover a large part of the requisites of the critical profession, especially in its earlier labours. It is not assumed that there are no other elementary processes which belong to the formation of critical opinion, particularly as giving it a personal and individual tone. But the critic who is looking for the principles which shall be to him what integrity and honesty are to the business man's career will not go far astray if he accept the foregoing principles as the fundamental laws and the governing motives of his professional labour. He will endeavour to make his knowledge adequate to the subject before him, his judgment as impersonal as justice itself, and his pronouncements above the imputation of fear or favour.

Such standards may be regarded as too exalted for every-day criticism, but they are not for the criticism of life in courts of law and on the judge's bench. If "literature is the criticism of life," as it has been frequently termed, then judgment pronounced upon it should come from a superior tribunal, which should base its decisions on the highest principles of justice and equity, and be actuated in its dealings by motives higher even than those which are expected to prevail in other forms of literature. If it is not governed by these higher motives, it must itself expect to be called to account by a supreme court which is always in session—the dominant sentiment of the best in any age, which pronounces its verdict after more formal tribunals have declared their own with greater or less conformity to absolute justice. It is this standard of truth and equity, varying from age to age, but always the highest standard in any age, by which the validity of all others is tested, and the value of all literary work estimated. Critical performance does not escape the unspoken judgment of the ruling thought in a thinking and reflective time; and

though it is a difficult matter to discover motives, and a delicate one to impute them, it is
probable that people will continue to exercise
the private right of conjecture on all subjects
that interest them, the undercurrents of criticism among the rest.

III

STANDARDS OF CRITICISM

"Seriously, there appears a need of some authority in criticism more patent to the public than the mere signature of one man or another."—ANONYMOUS.

WHEN criticism is limited to judgment pronounced by one person upon the work of others, the inquiry will naturally be raised, Upon what authority do his decisions rest, and what is its source ? If the answers to this question be diverse, how shall their complexity be simplified and some general agreement arrived at ? These two questions need replies before satisfactory statements can be made as to the standards of criticism. A backward look may be of service. Down to a recent time the opinion has prevailed that there are laws of literary composition observed by the best writers whose taste has led them to conform consciously or unconsciously to corresponding principles. The application varies according to the kind of writing, but among the more general are such as Unity, Adaptation, Grouping, Repetition, Diversity, Growth, and Emphasis.

Standards first based upon laws of composition.

Certain precepts of less importance or narrower application have also been observed, as a conciliatory disposition by speakers, and an interesting manner of writing by essayists, and by dramatists and novelists a treatment of the subject in a way to absorb attention early and keep it to the end. Other matters, such as whether or not the issue of plots should leave a pleasant feeling in the minds of readers, or a story should have a purpose, have been considered debatable. But a few main principles like those mentioned above have always been regarded as constituting a sort of unwritten compact or constitution in the republic of letters. No writer of note has attempted to violate its main provisions. If he has, his production has not long survived the attempt.

Early criticism based its judgments upon these principles, and compared literary performances with its standards. For more than a century before the establishment of the British Reviews it was the fashion to follow Anglo-Gallic principles of taste introduced into England at the Restoration. These were based upon a sentiment which maintained that the imitators of the ancients were the best modern writers. In accordance with this Classical standards. opinion, early criticism sought to deduce rules from the classics by which it should be guided in its estimates. It did not assume to pass judgment and decide questions of taste on its personal authority alone. Not until the days of Rymer and Dennis did critics in England set themselves up as judges of composition, independent of its laws, and as directors of authors. The earliest British criticism drew its principles and standards from works which were produced when there was little written criticism. Its doctrine was that the laws of judging are received from authors able to give them by their conformity to the fitness of things, and that the critic must gather from authors his notions of excellence. Or if he did not, there was a convenient theory that corresponding notions existed of necessity in the mind of a first-class critic. At a later day Coleridge more sensibly held to fixed canons of criticism deduced from the nature of man, as Dryden had before him, and called it arrogance to announce one's self to men of letters as a guide to their taste and judgment without reference to such a code. Burke declared that he could judge but poorly of anything while he measured it by no other standard than itself. The neglect of the ancient classics, Schopenhauer believes, will tend to a degeneration of the literature of criticism, and Lowell, remarking that the stamp of the Greeks is upon all the allowed weights and measures of criticism, adds, that " unless we admit certain principles as fixed beyond question we shall be able to render no adequate judgment, but only to record our own impressions, which may be valuable or not." [1]   It is asserted to the credit of M. Brunetière, that he has given back to the word " critic " something of its former meaning, that is, of one who has ideal convictions and insists on judging in accordance with them.   An American critic [2] remarks most sensibly: " Few of us deny that literary art has some permanent laws and standards.   The slow consensus of the best opinion rallies round works which obey these laws and conform to these standards, as did those classics which always appeal to mankind's deepest feeling for truth and beauty, and thus have stood the test of time."   It is the permanent element in these, separated from whatever was temporary and local, that can safely be taken as a stand-

[1] *Essays,* iii., 29, 34.
[2] Richard Burton

ard.   To this element whatever is likely to live will be found to conform in essential particulars.

Early in this century a departure from the absolutism of classical standards took place. Jeffrey and the *Edinburgh Review*, of which he was the first editor, mark the transition to a more personal standard; and also an appeal from the dogmatism of one man, which had sometimes been accepted as authority— Dr. Johnson's, for example—to that of several. Sensible of his own importance, and confident in his own personal competence as judge, he yields a point in favour of his associates when he says, that " the taste of very good judges is necessarily the taste of a few persons eminently qualified by natural sensibility and long experience to settle matters of excellence in literature."   In this concession, however, he goes no further than the little band of associate judges, of whom he would not deny that he is chief.   Nothing is allowed to a jury of twelve laymen, nor to the popular voice, which at the time was proclaiming the arrival of a new and marvellous poet by the name of Walter Scott.   But to his praise be it remarked, that Jeffrey had begun to move away from the ancient autocracy of the old-fashioned critic, who was a law unto himself and everybody else besides. He got so far as to include in his coterie, first, Sydney Smith, Francis Horner, Lord Brougham, Elmsley and Hamilton, Thomson and Murray, Watt and Davy, fellow-contributors to the *Edinburgh Review*. Later, he learned to have some respect for Gifford of the *Quarterly* and his associates, Southey, Scott, Canning, Ellis, and Croker, as well as for the contributors to other reviews and quarterlies of the time. Differ as he might from any or all of them on various points, he would admit that in matters of literary taste their judgment was worth considering, and that, taken together, their consensus of opinion was worth more than the pronouncement of any one of the number alone. Thus the authority of the feudal baron in letters began to be shared with neighbouring overlords in an oligarchy of taste and criticism.

It was an approach to a literary Academy in Great Britain, resembling the French Academy across the Channel as nearly as Matthew Arnold would have desired in his loyalty to British and personal independence. In any case, it had a strong sense of its corporate authority in matters of literary taste, and was never ambiguous in announcing its opinion of those who differed from it in theory or practice. Still it was the opinion of more than one person.   Or if any critic felt free to pass judgment as if he were the only one on the globe, any other of the little group might do the same, and thus modified verdicts became common.   There were a few instances where the rule of the Review-office gave colour to the literary opinions of subordinates, and still more to their political tenets, but no more than in the case of certain modern journals that might be mentioned.   At any rate, the authoritative decree of the dogmatic critic began to have less terrors than in the days of Ralph Griffiths, bookseller, and an editor in the interest of his own shop—a man who could command one of his henchmen to write down a book of Goldsmith's because the needy poet failed to pay a tailor's bill for which the autocrat editor had become security.   Such were possible canons of criticism in the age of dictatorships a century ago.

Since this first break with the methods of antiquity by Jeffrey and his colleagues, the criteria of taste have been broadened *Criteria broadened.* by wider and wider circles of judges competent to do justice to their vocation, and generally willing.   The tests applied by them have become more flexible, because multiplicity tends to catholicity, and Procrustean measurements are impossible with a many-minded

3

court of literary law. Still, codes of criticism, if they could be reduced to definite form, would not be found to vary so much among different nations as their civil codes.

At the present time it is probable that the phrase in Arnold's definition of criticism is doing something to determine the standard with which all literary work is to be compared,—" the best that is known and thought in the world."

There will, of course, always be a contention about what is best, as is evident from the diversified lists of the " hundred best books." But in them all ten will usually be found, to which the suffrages both of general readers and of scholars will unite in giving a majority vote. Intelligent people do not leave Chaucer and Spenser, Shakespeare and Milton out of the company of poets, nor Bunyan, Defoe, De Quincey, Scott, Macaulay, Ruskin, Carlyle, and Newman out of their choice of prose-writers, however many more they may include. Besides, there are later writers who are contributing to the sum of the best in fields which were not much cultivated in former centuries, notably the domain of science. This aggregate of " the best " is accordingly getting to be considerable in volume in every department of literature. It is also building up standards with which each new contribution can be compared in certain main particulars, after making deductions for variations in time and place of authorship. Thus the element of change by growth in standards will never be lost sight of. For example, there are features in the work of the Elizabethan dramatists that need not enter into dramatic composition at the present day. They would rightly be regarded as in bad taste. These are accidents of a ruder age than ours, and concessions to a noisy pit. But in the great essentials of the Romantic Drama no company of writers has reached a higher level than the men who used to assemble at the Mermaid Tavern. Certainly they can furnish more points to playwrights of our time than these seem able to imitate. The same may be said of old-fashioned Sir Walter with respect to the later novelists, and John Milton is still waiting for his successor in Epic poetry.

It would be asking too much of the reader to examine, and perhaps of the writer to state, the essential particulars which re- **Particular** main after eliminating the accidental **elements of** and temporary elements from the **permanence.** best that has been written and thought. But an example or two will illustrate what is meant by abiding and unchangeable principles of the best composition upon which standards

of criticism are based.   The authors just mentioned, each in his time and way, exemplified
such cardinal principles.   The chief of these
is the one which makes the best literature to
record life in the truest manner and in the
clearest form.

Fidelity in representation and transparency
in communication are essential qualities.   Loyalty to life and to the reader's ready
understanding will commend itself to
all as a standard to which the writer
will try to attain, and with which the
critic will compare any work before him.   If
it mirrors the experiences which befall mankind
with such exactness that the reader feels that his
own life, whether of action or of thought, has
been photographed, and if this representation
is as definite to his understanding and as easily
apprehended as a strong picture, then he may
be sure that two qualities of the best that has
been written are before him, namely, accuracy
and vividness of presentation.   If also the
thought is of the best, either in respect to its value to others or in its
rarity or profundity, then another quality has
been found which belongs to the highest grade
of literature, that is, exceptional thought.
Taken together, the two excellences of life-
like presentation and noble thought are the

first of the essential elements in the standard with which the critic will compare any composition according to its kind.

There are other qualities also. Literary art is one of them, that is, something which includes, but is also more than, faithful representation. For there are at *Literary art.* least two ways of telling the truth or communicating a fact. Very few are so fond of an unwelcome message as to have it told in the bluntest way, while ordinary information or a commonplace statement may be conveyed in such terms that its manner of communication will make it as agreeable as the new knowledge. As with any other deed, the grace with which it is done may be of more account than the act itself. Thus it comes about that even disagreeable truths and events and situations can be communicated, narrated, and described in such terms as to give pleasure in one way and another. This is the fundamental principle of literary art. He who knows how to employ it possesses what is called the literary faculty. He who perceives it has the critical sense. It is that adroitness which makes the most of the commonplace, clothes the ordinary event in interesting garb, and makes attractive the everyday occurrence. It can even disguise the disagreeable fact with insinuating form, and make that to be endured and harboured which in itself is repellent.

In general, the outcome of this quality is termed Style, although this includes something

Style.

more than an arrangement of words and phrases. Many writers upon literature make this feature its conserving power, the salt which keeps wealth of thought, originality of ideas, and even ethical truths, from neglect and waste and loss. Certainly it does much for uninteresting material which would otherwise be passed by, and adds to what is interesting the charm of adornment. It is the same as with man and his clothing. No doubt an Apollo in rags would be an Apollo still, but at a disadvantage. Clothed in raiment that becomes him, something is added. The main question is, What is becoming ? As in a statue, itself beautiful, that which least obscures its beauty is fitting, so it may be with the drapery of a noble thought. Absolute simplicity may then be best; the simplicity of Nature clothed with forests on the mountains, with grass on the meadows, with mist on the lakes, and with clouds in the sky,—grandeur, breadth, vastness, robed in transparency and light. But if there be uncouth, disordered, or decaying features, Nature takes great pains to compensate for the ungainly and uncomely by profuseness of growth and colour,—rank weeds to hide the scars by flood, luxuriant vines and foliage over dead trees and rocks and the ruined castles of men, most like her own architecture. So there are ideas so uncouth, fragmentary, or old as to need a wealth of ornamentation akin to the gorgeousness and pomp with which Nature clothes her harsher features, thus " giving them the greater honour." In both these ways, then,—by the inherent and unadorned beauty of a noble thought, and by the verbal clothing of it in profusion of grace bestowed lavishly upon the commonplace or the disagreeable,—does the literary art called Style make itself a large factor in the standard by which any author is to be judged.

There have been great stylists in sufficient abundance to furnish concrete examples of such standards of judgment, each for his own time and in some respects for all time. Homer and Dante, Shakespeare and Milton are the immortals in poetry who are always first recalled. Together they furnish an assemblage of perfections varied enough to satisfy the most fastidious. In prose, Bacon, De Quincey, Ruskin, Pater, Froude, Newman, and Lang will be reckoned among the essayists. In fiction, a still later form of literature in its higher grades, Hawthorne and Stevenson have exemplified the possibilities of language to portray the thoughts of the heart, and to depict the surroundings and scenes and experiences of human life. Some things, doubtless, were lacking in these great composers of later harmonies between thought and its expression, but each one made rare music on his own harp or viol; and together they constitute a choir unsurpassed since classic ages, and having a wider range than the Greeks themselves. Therefore the critic need not, as some would say, take the modern book back to the ancient to get its dimensions by the Hellenic or Latin measurement. Nor, again, admirable as it is for computation, need he go to France for the metre and the kilogram with which to gauge and estimate productions of authors who write the English language and think Anglo-Saxon thoughts. In their own tongue, on English and American soil, among their own people and kindred, critics in either nation may find standards of measurement which are exact sections of a longitudinal degree, and therefore of the equatorial circumference of the globe itself. Athens, Rome, and Paris are good meridians for their own surveyors to start from as from so many literary centres of the world; but they cannot render similar service to the English-speaking peoples. Right here at home, or among our kinsmen over the sea, are masters of every literary art with whom any aspirant to honour, fame, or immortality in letters may be compared, or to whose class he may be assigned by the inductive process, if the judicial be discarded.

These standards, representing the best that has been thought and written, and being within easy reach, ought to be a formative influence in every critic's judgment. This implies not so much wide reading on his part as diligent study and some care as to what he shall become most familiar with. It may also demand some self-denial. For if he prefer to read the light literature of the present day rather than the substantial and standard works of former times, or those of our own time which are likely to rank with them, he will not be able to pass judgment on these last. His capacity to understand and his ability to estimate will be limited to that with which he is best acquainted. He may be a connoisseur of books in paper covers, but not of books in boards. Or among the multitude of these his scales of justice may be graded to grains and scruples rather than to pounds and tons. The same book may likewise be of more value to one than another; and as it belongs to a class of its own, so it will find its own class of readers. The critic who is both inductive and judicial will assign it a place and its rank in that place. To do so his reading will have been wide enough to make him acquainted with leaders in the several departments of literature, and with some who are not. Between the best and the worst he will find little difficulty in rating any production at its approximate value.

The specialist critic will have done enough reading in his department to be saved further preparation. His task will be mainly one of grading. To this he will add specifications of excellence where it is found, and also of indifferent work or worse if it appears, since even the best writers cannot maintain uniform values and interest from beginning to end. It is not best that they should. The critic should recognise this law of unequal performance, and instead of dwelling upon the lower levels as blemishes, he should regard them as following the custom of Creation in making the valley contribute to the apparent height of the mountain. The level plane of a railway bed is the least interesting view in a landscape where ravines may be as picturesque or as restful as the towering hills.

It would be granting to criticism more of

concord than belongs to it if some notice were not taken of the element of scepticism in this matter of standards. The whole the-ory of Impressionism must be re-garded as opposed to external scales of measurement. The man who makes his own views the thumb-rule of estimating literary values of course needs no other rule. But there are great critics who say with M. Anatole France that there is " no ideal standard to which they may refer either their own opinions or those of other men." Another insists that the relative has taken the place of the absolute in criticism, and that the progressive nature of the laws of composition involve changes in critical taste in successive ages, and that the criteria of criticism change with the process of centuries. At present the drift is away from principles based upon ancient models, so far as they are peculiar to antiquity, toward laws derived from our common nature, modified by present conditions of life and thought and expression. But for standards which shall be permanent, reference must be had to that which has always been true of our common nature, and which always will be true of it. The personal standard must differ with different persons, and the historic with different times and nations; but underneath the turbulence or placidity of the surface, in storm or in calm, unvarying currents are always moving. With them the greater movements in literature go in various guise in every generation; and after them, or as one of them, criticism must follow, if it is to be anything more than an ephemeral and perishable form of literature.

IV

DIVERSITY IN CRITICISM

"Critics still argue and the court's in doubt."—HORACE.

IF the sole authority for every critic is to be his own judgment, it is plain that the one thing which will belong to all criticism will be its diversity. Given the individual idiosyncrasy and the feeling of personal independence, there is nothing left to secure uniformity and agreement in judg- *Independence breeds diversity.* ment except such general views as belong to a common human nature. Now and then it will happen that two persons take the same view, but differences will not be diminished as the number of critics begins to multiply. Again, a book will strike some prevailing sentiment or common sympathy, and elicit a favourable response from an entire class or community. This has been the case with works written in the interest of reform when the popular mind was ripe for it. But when the occasion has passed, and the volume can be examined as literature, a growing difference of critical opinion often ensues. The most widely read American book of the last half-century is an instance of this. There was a time when a critic would have risked his reputation for sound judgment if he had admitted that there could be literary blemishes in a work which went with the current of half a nation's sentiment, and helped to swell and hasten its movement. It has now taken its place with the writings of the nineteenth century, and a generation has arisen to judge it as literature which can never know the power with which it came to the fathers. There is the same diversity of verdict as in the instance of all books that attract wide attention. Some say one thing and some another about them, and no two exactly agree. How can they when their angle of vision in material objects is never identical ?— and many more causes of variation enter into the mental vision than into the bodily. Looking at a cathedral a traveller may call to his companion to admire a certain arch, buttress, or pinnacle, and get the answer back, that his friend cannot see it from where he stands, or that there is no line of beauty in it from his point of view. When this one has stood in the other's tracks he sees it as the first one saw it.

The difference in this instance is readily and easily removed. It is a still more difficult undertaking to get another into one's intellectual footprints. Or if this is accomplished, there are peculiarities of mental eyesight to be considered, and beyond these, diversities of taste, so that impressions will differ in literary things vastly more than in those belonging to any other art. It is a rare couple for whom the same field-glass does not have to be adjusted to a different focus as it passes from hand to hand. Then there is sometimes a little vanity in differing, and in seeming to have a mind of one's own, or in the fear lest one shall not be thought to have personal views and opinions, or again a natural love of differing from others and of taking always the opposition bench.

There are also differences among critics from principle, so called. The utterance of one school or party is the immediate incentive to the other to pronounce an opposite verdict and in so far to reverse the decision of the first, and incidentally, to show its defective judgment; for critics are a class not wholly at peace with all who draw the claymore. It is an uncommon provocation that will unite in confederacy all the tribes which wear a tartan, with never a MacDonald or MacGregor standing out for his own opinion against all comers.   Even martyrdom for singularity has its compensations.

From these and similar causes criticism comes to have great variety in its character. Its current record in any year is the best proof of this.   Those who watch the appreciations, or lack of them, on the appearance of any new book will sometimes be bewildered in attempting to gather the prevailing sentiment in regard to it. One notice calls it good, another indifferent, still another, poor stuff.   The reader or buyer would be puzzled did he not cherish a profound confidence in himself or his favourite journal in matters literary as well as political and religious.   Often he may see no other Review than his own, and thus fail to add to his stock of accepted truths this one about the possible disagreements among good judges of literary products.   He will at least have comfortable convictions, undisturbed by counter opinions. A wider reader's convictions may be less assuring, and more composite in their character. He will recall the trite proverb concerning tastes and disputing about them.

For a completer acquaintance with diversities of criticism one may be referred to authors,

who are apt to note them.   With the facilities
furnished by the clipping bureaus their knowledge in this direction is limited only
by the amount of subscription paid,   Authors'
and by the extent to which opinions   of diversity
have been printed.   Aside from the   in criticism.
publisher, probably no one is a better authority
on variations in critical vision than the writer
whose aftermath consists of daily cuttings from
the book columns of newspapers and periodicals.   It may become a subject for wager, as
in dull days at sea, from which quarter critical
winds will blow next, and whether fair or foul,
and how many knots will be run.   Sometimes
the run will be free and breezes propitious for
days together, and then a spell of weather fall,
or cloud and sunshine may alternate with shifty
irregularity.   Such was seemingly the case
with the author who published his experience
in the nineteenth volume of *Current Literature*, pp. 297–8.   He says:

" I wrote a novel, and then I subscribed shekels
to a press agency for all reviews of the book which
should appear. ' I don't expect many favourable
notices,' I lied to myself, ' but at least I shall learn
my faults and failings,' and it was in this humble
mood that I read what my critics had to say. Of
the book as a whole I learned as follows :
4

"'Why was it written? As a novel it is dull; the dialogue is tedious, and the book a bore.'—*Catholic World*.

"'To be commended from several points of view, but one could box the compass without occasion for finding fault.'—*Philadelphia Ledger*.

"'Every page, every line, is full of interest.'—*Detroit Free Press*.

"'The end is very long in coming.'—*New Haven Register*.

"'The dramatic interest never flags.'—*Independent*.

"'There are some striking improbabilities.'—*Peoria Standard*.

"'There is no improbability about the story.'—*Atlantic Monthly*.

"'The story is long and dull.'—*Book News*.

"'There is not a dull or stupid page in the book.'—*San Francisco Chronicle*.

"I looked over the critiques for the comments on the subject of the book, if not on the novel as a whole, to read :

"'The author evidently knows New York politics thoroughly.'—*San Francisco Chronicle*.

"'The hero is typical of nothing in New York politics.'—*Hartford Post*.

"'Impossible in real life.'—*Minneapolis Tribune*.

"'Reads like the actual history of certain political movements.'—*Literary World*.

"'The hero could not have done anything of the sort in real life.'—*Chicago Tribune*.

"'There is not an experience the author writes about that has not happened.'—*N. Y. Times.*"

In regard to the characters, the author found the following diverse opinions of the press:

"'[The hero is] a commonplace, mawkish, stupid goody-goody chump. He is simply an old-fashioned idiot.'—*Chicago Herald.*

"'One of the strongest and most vital characters that have appeared in our fiction.'—*The Dial.*

"'Too priggish, and not original.'—*New Haven Register.*

"'The most attractive, manly, and lovable hero.'—*Detroit Free Press.*

"'The heroine was n't worth marrying or writing about.'—*Milwaukee Sentinel.*

"'[The writer] has drawn an attractive young girl—a most difficult performance.'—*The Critic.*

"'The hero with a horror of silliness and detail proceeds to fall in love.'—*Chicago Herald.*

"'A very charming love story.'—*The Dial.*"

After contemplating this instance of uniformity and agreement in criticism the author naturally is led to ask: "Which half of the critics read my book, and which half did n't?" He might also have asked: "Which of them read half the book and which the whole of it; which read the preface only, and which only the title-page?"

Sometimes a seeming diversity of opinion is made a cloak for a pronounced sentiment by a single reviewer.   Such an one is mentioned by the editor of the *Fortnightly Review* : " He begins by crowning me with garlands and fillets, and bedewing me with odours, but speedily proceeds to knock me on the head with his pole-axe." Every reader of the *Sketch-Book* will recall Irving's closing page, added to the second London edition, in which he acknowledged his critics to be

" a singularly gentle and good-natured race who each in turn had objected to some one or two articles, amounting in the aggregate to almost a total condemnation of his work ; but then he has noticed that what one has particularly censured another has particularly praised. . . . For a time he determined to govern himself in his second volume by the opinions passed upon the first ; but one advised him to avoid the ludicrous ; another to shun the pathetic ; a third assured him that he was tolerable at description, but cautioned him to leave narrative alone ; a fourth declared that he had a very pretty knack at turning a story, and was really entertaining when in a pensive mood, but was grievously mistaken if he imagined himself to possess a spirit of humour."

In view of this diversity of judgment he concludes to go on in his own way. The judgment of half a century has approved of his decision.

Possibly, however, criticism is doing more service to literature by reason of its variety than it could by uniformity. It indicates the completer view which can be taken by many persons, and should accordingly be more satisfactory to one who is looking for the whole truth. If he finds nothing but the truth he will be fortunate and ought to be contented. Owing to the imperfection of critical eyesight and of the media it often looks through, absolute accuracy cannot always be expected. Personal equations must be reckoned with, prejudices allowed for, partial knowledge considered. On the other hand, each examiner finds an excellence or an imperfection that escapes the rest, and the average opinion can be gathered as other averages are computed. The result will usually be like that which belongs to all mundane performance—good, bad, and indifferent in varying proportions.

Next to the author such diversity in judgment must have its instruction for critics themselves. One who has great confidence in his personal insight and acumen cannot but receive a little shock to his critical sensorium when he reads a condemnatory review by his respected neighbour over the way of a book which he has just commended to all readers. In effect such opposite views are a criticism of his own literary perceptions and taste, a critique in advance upon himself, his theories, and methods. Of course he may retaliate by pronouncing the other defective in taste and judgment, or for once wofully mistaken. Nevertheless he may not be quite easy in mind and assured of his own infallibility. Certainly he will not believe that the entire brotherhood enjoys immunity from errors when still other diversities of opinion are read. Authors who have suffered many things from critics would have their sweet revenges if they could see what these judges of theirs endure at each other's hands in their daily work. If one man were as good as another, and his opinion worth as much, there would be no friction and no chagrin; but, unfortunately, there are grades in this hierarchy, known to those within its ranks, with the usual respect for the exalted and deference to their decisions. Accordingly the hasty reviewer who has run amuck of the deliberate and almost infallible judge will have dismal searchings of heart when he sees what he ought to have said in the *American Eagle* printed in the *Literary Law Reporter*. Or else he will console himself with the dogma that every man has a right to his own opinion, and that personal independence and self-sufficiency are the foundation and stronghold of all criticism. Happy is the critic who can thus comfort himself!

Happier, however, is that author whom all critics delight to honour. This is not an unheard-of occurrence. At rare intervals some writer commands the almost unqualified approval and commendation of all or nearly all whose literary judgment is worth the most. Their occasional agreement in such instances constitutes an element of confidence and hope in this branch of literature. It indicates that the best judges know the best work, and have the grace to recognise it publicly. In doing this they help establish the confraternity of letters, and show that they are not all or always Ishmaelites, whose hand is against every man, and, by consequence, every man's hand against them. They become by such generous dealing accepted and acceptable members in the brotherhood of literary workers, and are to be welcomed as benefactors and helpers in the guild of letters. This is as true when judicious qualification is mingled with approbation as when the praise is unalloyed. The right-minded author will accept such appreciation in the spirit in which it is given—for the advancement of good literature. He will take graciously any suggestions that put him in the way of making contributions to it. But he will naturally look for those particulars in which the majority agree, rather than for the exceptional and one-sided strictures which proceed from abnormal idiosyncrasy, prejudice, or ignorance.

It is such minor personal views that most contribute to the diversities of criticism. It is true here, as in graver matters, that men differ more in their opinions than in radical beliefs. Modes and methods are oftener grounds of controversy than the object and purpose of literature. The poetic diction of Ruskin, the antitheses of Macaulay, the oracles of Emerson, are as a wall between the small-minded critic and the larger purpose and motive of these authors. Once bring him to see the deeper design and the personality of the writer, and the individual style and method will seem the only possible channel in which the thought could run for that particular thinker. Make an interchange of manner, let one write in the style of another, and the outcry against the accidents of composition would be louder than it now is against personal peculiarities and apparent defects.

In spite, however, of the little angularities which inexperienced judgment seizes upon, there comes at length the agreement of the wiser to place genius and talent where they belong. The classics, which no one thinks of criticising to-day as recent compositions are judged, had their time of cavil from petty penny-a-liners. Milton was slow in coming to recognition, Shakespeare slower still, after two generations of partial appreciation. Wordsworth and his neighbour bards attained such eminence as is now granted them through much critical tribulation. Tennyson and our own Longfellow did not escape the critical cranks of their time. A later time came for them all, the time of oblivion for the gad-fly and of enthronement for the genius it tried to sting; and also of endorsement for the higher appreciation by the bolder few who ventured to recognise talent in a contemporary in the midst of general dispraise.

It may, then, be safely concluded that diversity in criticism of the best literature is one of its accidental features, destined to disappear or at least to diminish as years go by. Time brings settled and uniform judgments, precipitating substances that cloud, and leaving clarified convictions in the mind of suc-

ceeding generations.   The author becomes
either a standard or a relic.   Sometimes a rash
spirit, " tired of hearing Aristides called the
Just," attempts to upset the accepted opinion,
and reverse the decisions of ages; but the end
of that man is near.   He is regarded as a
curious reversion to a forgotten type of reviewer, a back number out of his grandfather's
garret, a descendant of some carping caviller
in a remote century, an Aristarchus sitting in
judgment upon Homer.

How much may be done toward eliminating
differences in criticism by sincere endeavour to
make it conform to truth and justice is seen by
comparing the work of the best.   How much
also may be done to multiply this diversity
is apparent from the superficial, haphazard,
flippant pronunciamentos of those who are too
indolent to inform themselves, or too incompetent to discover what is best in a book.   For
the poorest they have an affinity, like flies for
rottenness, and fasten on it and dwell upon it
and magnify it until a reader would suppose
the volume was nothing but a comedy of errors
and ignorance.   Whatever is good in it they
have no use for, since it requires gifts of appreciation with which they are not endowed.
As a consequence they go on contributing to
the diversity of criticism its most unfortunate

factors, and in so far adding to the disrepute it has fallen into by similar exploits heretofore.

What has been said about diversity is not to be taken as denying that there may be valid reasons for difference of opinion among eminent critics as among eminent judges on the bench. This would be to refuse both individuality and independence to literary judgment. A reader of critical literature will be impressed with these two features of it at an early day. One such reader, himself a critic, makes it an ordinary perception that " critical literature is made up in large part of conflicting judgments . . . often arbitrary and unexplained." [1] He furnishes an example in the opposing opinions of Mr. Swinburne and Mr. Leslie Stephen regarding Rochester as a study of masculine character in *Jane Eyre*. Similar disagreement can be found by the diligent searcher in regard to the principal characters of every prominent novelist. They impress one and another as differently as persons in real life impress this one and that one. In larger matters there are the same differences to be accounted for on the same principle of human diversity,—questions that always will be considered open to controversy, because the variety of views is great

[1] J. M. Robertson, *Essays*, p. 117.

among authorities of equal value. The meaning of literature and its definite province, the
relation of the intellectual element in poetry
to the impassioned, the classification of literary periods, the rank of fiction, and the possible underestimate of prose as compared with
verse, are among the unsettled literary prob-
lems which Professor Hunt enumerates.[1] If
there are diverse opinions in such questions,
there must also be upon less important ones,
as those with respect to the rank of rival
authors and their productions, or to a present
fashion in letters compared with a past, or to
this year's crop of fiction outmeasuring last
year's. But to abolish diversity itself means a
reconstruction of human nature, and of the
natural world, to whose variety many differences of mental constitution may be traced.

There are still smaller questions over which
critics sometimes wrangle, and dilettanteism
Differences about trifles. fidgets with its '' little bundle of
quisquilious jottings,'' pestering
authors now and then like sand in the shoes.
Whereas, both authors and readers might get
a little incidental comfort out of these disagreements if they would. The author will see that
all the army cannot be as one man against him
when divided against itself. He may even

____
[1] *Studies in Literature and Style*, p. 292.

take grim satisfaction in calling to mind the proverbial instability of houses so divided, and thus account for the otherwise unexplained inefficiency of such households. Meantime the reader, perplexed in proportion as he consults authorities, may be forced back upon his own judgment in choosing between critics. Or better, he may bravely determine to do his best as an independent judge, thus becoming himself an impressionist critic before he is aware of what he has unwittingly accomplished. For those who have a more distant outlook and larger hopes for the millennium of critical unity, there is the slow-forming consensus of time. This is the final arbiter and conserver of what is most permanent amidst and throughout all the fickle and ephemeral aspects which literature assumes as an outer garment with the changing seasons and the passing generations. Underneath their needful and pleasing diversity is the body of literature which is more than its raiment, and the life which outlasts all changes of fashion, and the spirit which pervades differing and alterable customs. About these enduring elements there will never be much diversity of the best judgment, since their identity is recognised under varying costumes century after century.

V

PHASES OF CRITICISM

"It is hard to find a whole age to imitate, or what century to propose for example."—SIR THOMAS BROWNE.

IT would be singular if there were no advancement in the learning which has been an observer of the progress of literature during twenty centuries and more. Change in its methods might be expected corresponding with the varying aspects of composition. These themselves might have differed more if certain eminent standards, called classic, had not been recognised and followed generation after generation. To their influence, and especially to that of classical critics, must be credited a remarkable continuance of primitive methods and ruling ideas in judgment of literary composition. When, however, it is asserted, with justice, that there was little improvement for ages in the critical art, the retort is obvious that there were periods long after the classic which could not show any other than a retrograde movement in general literature. The uncritical achievements of mediæval scholars were only a poor imitation of antiquity. Yet they had the sense to admit an excellence which they could not rival, and to respect most profoundly an art to which they could not attain. Their hospitality toward the classics was undiscriminating.

As has already been intimated, the general character of early criticism grew out of this profound respect for classical literature. Beginning with the inductions of the first great critical analyst, Aristotle, this basis of judgment held sway down to a comparatively recent date, even as the works of the Stagirite himself on Rhetoric and Poetic held their own in European universities far into the present century. Like Homer, he has been hard to get rid of. He has been translated and transformed, condensed, and diluted by turns, but his reproving ghost seems " doomed to walk the earth for a certain term, and clad in complete steel, revisit poor fools of nature "—as he would doubtless call some of his successors, in the same spirit which made him say that his predecessors had busied themselves most mightily with subordinate details of composition. Other and modifying agencies appeared from time to time increasing or diminishing the force of his code of criticism; notably the methods of Longinus and Cicero and Horace in Latin literature, and in its successors, the Romance. Throughout all the critical ages down to the days of Samuel Johnson the image and superscription of the great analyst is plain, or can easily be deciphered, upon the current coin of literary judgment. Personal departures are found here and there, and changes by reason of intellectual driftings and fashions. Still the course of criticism is marked out with tolerable definiteness. In the main, it runs along the line of classic authority with more or less artificiality of rule; as, for instance, in the matter of the three unities, which used to be considered the three graces of dramatic composition, but at length were discarded.

A devotee of the evolution theory would not find it difficult to discover another proof of its wide prevalence if he should trace the *Movements in criticism in* development of criticism, especially *the present century.* during the present century. If he should be puzzled by its slow advance in former times, he might be equally surprised by the rapidity of its movements within the last fifty years. It may not be that all forms of criticism which preceded this age were primordial — they certainly cannot be termed crude,—but an epoch in the history of the art lies somewhere in the orbit of this century. Its exact position and limits may not be known until more distant and clearer observations can be taken; but there are evidences that the formative processes of a new criticism have been going on and are still at work. Some may consider this movement only as a November meteoric shower of regular recurrence, which others, adhering to the Talmudic legend, will interpret as the throwing of stones by bad and spiteful angels. Still, that there is an unusual activity in critical spheres few will deny.

That there also prevails a larger and better spirit than of old all will admit. One need not look beyond the progress made in our own country for proof of this. Lowell truly says : " Of colonial criticism there was none, and what assumed its place was a half-provincial conceit, half-patriotic resolve to find swans in birds of quite another species." It is sixteen years since a writer,[1] who ought to know whereof he wrote, declared that " until the last thirty years nobody had ever dreamt that a critic ought to look at a book or author from anything higher

A larger spirit prevails; reasons for judgment.

[1] Grant Allen in *Fortnightly Review*, xxxvii., 342.

5

than his own immediate likes and dislikes."
This statement may need qualification, but certainly the time has now come when a man must
give reasons for the belief that is in him satisfactory to others, who may have in them an
equally strong belief running in an opposite
direction. Otherwise he is a private and not
an official. This is eminently true if novel or
radical views are broached. The discoverer of
a new truth or a new planet is heavily handi-
capped with a weighty burden of proof by the
multitude who are less fortunate in their quick-
ness of vision. Give us your reason, they
insist, not your word for it. Thus to the
catholicity which French criticism had reached
under Sainte-Beuve, allowing every man to
speak his mind, Brunetière has added the demand that it shall not outrage the " testimony
and experience of all men as embodied in tradition " or history. As a contemporary writer
has felicitously put it, the critic's obligation is
" to listen to the still, small voice within, and
also to the voice of time and authority; that is
the delicate and difficult business of the serious-
minded critic."

On the objective side there have been
similar changes for the better. Early criticism
busied itself with matters of form: words and
the choice of them, verse and the measures of

it, prose and its divisions, applications, and limitations. It was sometimes an affair of French gardening—squares, triangles, and circles were of more account than what grew in the plat. Something that could be trimmed was the main requisite for Gallic and Anglo-Gallic criticism in the days of Rapin and Bossu in France and of Dryden in England. It was much the same in Pope's day when Dennis and Kenrics and Ralph prescribed for authors right-angled rules of composition, and insisted upon form as the chief virtue of literature.

Moreover the form was by no means classic in an age of classicists, so called, but rather an arbitrary bondage to artificial fashions of constraint. Grace, simplicity, and power are as absent from the ideals of that age as the freedom and naturalness of a Greek frieze are from the bewigged and beruffled beaux and the powdered and patched dames who smirk at each other on the canvases of Sir Godfrey Kneller. Pope's *Essay on Criticism*, so quotable and generally sensible, is only a happy embodiment of current sentiments of the contemporaneous literary class and of club conversation. Judged by its purpose, in accordance with its own first canon, it answers the end for which it was written well

enough; but its standards were those of the ·
town and country readers who took the affable
Spectator with their breakfast and the vivacious
Guardian with their tea.   It is easy to imagine
the guest from Grub Street dropping in with a
copy of Horace in one pocket of his full-skirted
coat and the latest translation of Boileau in
the other.   He was the heir-presumptive of an
obsolescent classicism in criticism.

The romanticism which followed produced
little that was romantic in the judgment of it,
unless virulence on the one side and
endurance on the other constitute a
sort of Covenanter romance.   This need not be
touched upon again.   Its history has been
epitomised by one [1] who says:

Romanticism.

" It rested on the assumption that it was the
proper business of criticism between 1820 and 1825
not so much to display characteristic excellences
as to detect imperfections—to play, in short, the
judge's part in condemning, or, say, the police ser-
geant's part in apprehending, literary defaulters."

Still there had been a movement away from
classical authority and the dogmatism of the
autocrat, toward a sort of impressionism and
an oligarchy in judgment.   If it was a real advance, it was after the manner of a point on

[1] Hall Caine, *Cobwebs of Criticism.*

the circumference of a moving waggon-wheel, suggesting retrograde progress. Even this, however, was in conformity to the general course of all progressive movements. It served its turn in bringing the critical art to better things through disgust with the worse. A later criticism dropped the asperity and acerbity of the earlier part of the century, and adopted a new temper and juster standards.

For example, recent criticism does not, like that of Queen Anne's day or the third George's, set up a single author by which to measure all literature modern and ancient. Addison was like his age, and had his uses afterward ; but there have been better essayists than he, surpassing their teacher. Johnson's ponderous diction was improved upon by Burke and his associates; but the modern critic would not demand that either Daniel Webster or Demosthenes should be rated by the parliamentary eloquence of the reign of George the Third. Criticism would not now insist, as it did at the beginning of the century, that no poet should soar much above Dryden and Pope, nor any novelist surpass Fielding, Richardson, and Sterne. Not until Coleridge and his compeers gave some catholicity to the critical spirit, was there an emancipation from the hide-bound tyranny of a literary monometallism whose standard was not always gold. The movement toward a larger liberty, started by these pioneers in the face of ridicule and scorn, has nevertheless brought in a new era of literary judgment. Wider ranges of thought are recognised, deeper earnestness of motive, emotions more sincere and less noisy. Unrepressed by factitious laws, imagination has flown straight to its mark, and style has been enriched by the variety of demands upon expression consequent upon excursions into many lands. All this expansion the best criticism has approved more and more in the last threescore years. To the general improvement of critical methods the largest contributor was Carlyle, bringing as he did philosophy out of Germany to the aid of criticism. Following Fichte and Hegel and Goethe he made hitherto unheard-of inquiries about the history of the man who writes, his time, his dwelling-place, his neighbours, and his nation, and showed that the man of letters is the interpreter of his age and its tendencies, and that literature itself is a record of the evolution of one century from another. Thus Carlyle broadened the acreage of criticism a hundred-fold.

The notion that criticism is largely a fault-finding business was slow to die, as may be seen by its temper in the first quarter of this century. Of it one remarks who " spent three mortal months in its perusal with the inexpressible sense of its infelicity, blundering, and bad passions,—' the good books it assailed are not lost, and the bad ones it glorified do not survive.' " Neither does its temper survive, except in the hill-country of literature, always the last to yield to civilising influences. In its capitals a new spirit reigns. First, in the attention paid to thought and matter as distinguished from details of form. Character has become of more consequence than clothes. It is admitted that fashions must change, and that every fashion is the best one for the time that it lasts; that while the flowing simplicity of the old Greek costumes may best become ideal perfection of figure and a leisurely life in a climate not severe, it would hardly answer New England purposes the year round, day in and day out. Similar necessities are laid upon composition and the criticism of it. But there has always been such a thing as nobility of character under Greek peplum and Roman toga, the embroidered waistcoat of the French Empire, and the dress-suit which stands for the republican simplicity of America abroad and at home, whatever may be said about its essential beauty.

Criticism
emphasises
character.

The main thing, after all, which outlasts all the fashions and is recognised underneath any of them is the union of honourable traits that makes what is known as character with its various manifestations. Something akin to this is what the criticism that deserves the name is looking for in literature. Sterling thoughts which square with right ethical standards, having practical values for the uplifting of private views and public sentiment, and honest purposes for the elevation of life, and of literature as its portrayer and interpreter,—these are the elements for which a later criticism is looking. If it finds them it will approve them and thus approve itself. If it does not find them, it will condemn, and thus justify its own reason for existence. It will not be insensible to beauty of form, nor especially to its fitness to the temper of the time, but spirit will always be more than its manifestation. Like the inner principle of life everywhere, it will, if strong enough, clothe itself with a body that becomes its spirit, and is an outward symbol of its disposition and purpose. Even such are the literary styles of critics themselves, diverse as those of Jeffrey, Carlyle, and Lowell.

No one can be oblivious to the element of sympathetic interpretation which enters into recent criticism, as contrasted with the instinctive antagonism of an earlier time. Something more than the printed page is taken into account. This interpretation is larger than what is known as interpretative criticism by comparison. Carlyle marks the introduction of this feature into English critical literature in speaking of the insight into Roman life which Heyne had given in his edition of Virgil. " The circumstances in which the author wrote " have now come to be an indispensable part of the newer critic's knowledge. Matthew Arnold embodied the same idea in his " atmosphere," as also did Taine, by his own showing following the suggested system of Sainte-Beuve, in his method of studying every work as a product of three forces—the race, the environment, and the special influence of the age in which it was written. Other eminent critics are following these distinguished leaders into the wide domain opened by such a method. Minto and Lowell caught the spirit that was in the air and discussed the signs of the new world of criticism, and obeyed their instincts toward a theory as genial as it is just. M. Henequin, in his *Scientific Criticism*, insists upon three things: first, observing the way in which a writer produces his technical effect, by words, sentences, scenes, characters, and other details; next an analysis of his personality; and then a study of his readers and admirers. How much these elements have to do with the final estimate of a given author he has exemplified by an analytic and synthetic view of Victor Hugo's literary work, as quoted in Robertson's *New Essays towards a Critical Method*. The same author points out that Renouvier has gone beyond Henequin's explanation of Hugo's works to find what illumination he can from his personal biography.

Thus, step by step, has criticism advanced in its search for whatever can contribute to its ultimate judgment. From placing a book of poems by a copy of Homer, or of orations by the *Oration on the Crown*, or of essays by Bacon's, and testing the new by a rule of the old, it has come at last almost to a physical diagnosis of each author before pronouncing upon the place and value of his intellectual product. His inheritance from the past, his present environment, social, moral, and intellectual, his breathing and circulation even, all are elements in the latest calculations of criticism in France, where it is most scientific and most appreciated, and in England and America, which are adopting similar methods. Differences there are, as there will be in all achievements of great talent, but these differences are not like the distinction between it and the hack-work which is done in haste and carelessness. The tone of it also has improved as much as its methods of investigation. Contrast Taine with Jeffrey and Brunetière with Gifford and this end of the century reviewers in general with those at the other end of it. Advance in manner is equalled by improvement in manners. Meantime, nothing of effectiveness has been sacrificed. The keenness of a French pruning-knife is as efficient among the exuberant growths of literature as the British bush-hook of eighteen hundred and ten. Imagine any disciple of Sainte-Beuve saying :

"We wish we could entertain any tolerable hopes of converting this poet from the damnable heresies into which he has fallen, and to which, if he does not reform speedily, we fear his reputation will die a martyr. The poetry of the 'Lay' is beneath criticism ; it has all sorts of commonplace defects without any beauties. Does he think that he should be as old-fashioned in his language as in the cut of his clothes ? "

British critics, and American also, following French examples, have vastly improved in the minor ethics of civility and urbanity without losing their effectiveness.   This may be true of leaders only, but it was not true of the chiefs fourscore years ago.   If it is not true now of some journalistic criticism, it is perhaps the fault of those readers who have little relish for genuine appreciations and interpretations, and have considerable enjoyment of a more anti-quated style.   A critical writer[1] ascribes pre-sent reversions to a former type

"to poor pay, the necessity of consulting popular prejudices, and a general lack of the sense of re-sponsibility.   The critic is free to deal out, as a rule anonymously, not only praise and blame but insult, misrepresentation, opprobrium, ridicule ; and the extent to which he will pervert facts, words, and principles, to gratify a prejudice or a resent-ment, is an ugly thing to see when it does not set up an impression of mere childishness.   A judge on the bench is expected to put away the methods of his barrister days and to set up for himself an ideal of decent impartiality.   It is scarcely so with the average anonymous critic."

This is a grave impeachment to proceed from one of the craft who has the right to speak with authority to his juniors in age and experience.   If it is true, however, the repetiti-tion of it may help to hasten the more general

[1] J. M. Robertson.

prevalence of the better methods of a later criticism as practised by the best. It is certainly much pleasanter to discuss these than the " pagan creed outworn" of a century ago, which current criticism does not profess or generally follow.

The progress that has been made is a noticeable feature in these phases of criticism as they succeed one another. Literature is no longer estimated by a personal standard which each critic may choose to set up for himself and others to worship. *The progress in phases of criticism.* Not even a golden calf, molten out of the contributed appreciations and praises of the mixed multitude, can any longer be foisted upon them for their adoration. They have come to distrust themselves and leaders who yield to their clamours. They are learning to wait for the man who shall come down from the mount of contemplation with the tables of fundamental law. They have found that there are tests better and surer than popularity to apply to literary products, if permanence is to be considered; that a work must have an intimate relation to their life, and become the record and representative of it and their age to be worth anything to posterity. It must fall in with the organic growth of literature as the history of the race in order to be preserved as a part of that history and a reflection of it. In all this a forward movement is perceived, and the drift away from individual to scientific methods, in harmony with the spirit of modern thought in other departments of intellectual activity. Breadth of view and length of reach have supplanted narrowness and short-sightedness. Catholicity has taken the place of prejudice; comprehensiveness, of local and partisan likes and dislikes. The perception of a few underlying principles, themselves tending toward unity, is making criticism one of the sisterhood of sciences, and not merely an empirical art differing in its aims and methods with each practitioner. Instead, every critic who hopes to be rated as an authority will be drawn into the system which has gradually been arranging itself out of the nebulous brilliances or murky mists of ages gone by. Or else he may, if he prefer, take his chances as an eccentric body, subject to no regulation that has been discovered save the somewhat doubtful one of being a law unto one's self. This general movement toward system is also in harmony with the other toward unity and liberty under organic law. In them both there is hope for the best efficiency of criticism in the future.

VI

IMPRESSIONISM

" Non amo te, Sabidi, nec possum dicere quare ;
Hoc tantum possum dicere, non amo te."—MARTIAL.

THE term Criticism, even when cleared of the fault-finding significance of its colloquial use, has still considerable latitude of meaning. It is employed in all the length and breadth of the way from a *Criticism a comprehensive term.* newspaper book-notice up to the highest analysis and comparison of literary and artistic undertakings, not to mention philosophic and scientific achievements. In such a wide application there is much opportunity for ambiguity and consequent misunderstanding. As a precaution against such misinterpretation something should be said defining the relative position and value of different kinds of criticism. This will be undertaken in two general classes—what may be called the ordinary or common and the higher or philosophical forms of literary criticism.

To begin with the simplest kind, which belongs to every reader who has any thought Orders of critics. about what he reads. His standard of judgment is what he likes or dislikes. This standard varies with education, inheritances, and surroundings. It cannot always be accounted for by the reader himself. As Thomas Brown,[1] satirist upon everybody and Dryden in particular, quaintly and honestly remarked, deftly turning an epigram of Martial's:

> " I do not love thee, Doctor Fell,
> The reason why I cannot tell ;
> But this alone I know full well,
> I do not love thee, Doctor Fell."

It is the child's universal reason—" Because." Because of what, nine persons out of ten may not be able or willing to explain. Still, they are ready to pronounce sentence according to their feelings and impressions.

A step beyond are the people who are able to give one good reason why they like this or dislike that. One might say that the thrill of horror in a ghost story gave him a not unpleasant " creepy " sensation, or that a certain rhyme pleased his sense of jingle, or a well-turned sentence his ear for rhythm. In any of

[1] 1663-1704.

these instances there may be other and higher
reasons for genuine admiration which wholly
escape the undeveloped critical sense of the
second class of readers.

In the third class is found one who can give
two or three reasons for his delight or disgust.
But they are his alone, shared by no one else
perhaps. By these instances one might be led
to accept a recent definition of criticism, " that
in its widest meaning it is nothing more than
judgment and decision, and that as a consequence all readers are critics." Coleridge puts
it in another way: " And now all men being
supposed able to read, the multitudinous public, shaped into personal unity by the magic of
abstraction, sits nominal despot on the throne
of criticism." [1] Its qualifications for the position he compares to those of St. Nepomuc who
was installed guardian of bridges, because he
had fallen off one and sunk out of sight!

The enumeration of grades might go on in a
narrowing circle until at last a man should be
found who gets beyond the personal standard
of his private sentiments. Upon him has
dawned the possibility of standards which exist
independent of individual preferences. He
confesses that there may be certain broad and
well defined principles prevailing in the domain

[1] *Biographia Literaria*, chap. ii.

of judgment,—principles which have been established by the concurrent voice of those whose attainments entitle them to speak authoritatively. What these principles are will then become a matter of inquiry, and the critic's eminence as an authority will depend upon his success in searching, followed by a corresponding fidelity to these standards when once discovered.

Thus the progression advances from the casual reader up to the one who passes judgment as he reads and gives the grounds of his decisions to himself at least—grounds which will stand the test of fundamental law above and beyond private considerations. In this category may be found an entire community of judges, ranging like a corresponding order in civil courts from the justice of the peace up to the bench of a nation's highest tribunal; from the apprentice piecing out a short column with a book-notice due the publisher, up to the accomplished Unknown who discovers where a book's strong and weak points are by the intuition of critical acumen approaching genius.

As there are grades of critics ranging from private readers up to professional judges of literature, so there are corresponding degrees of criticism, advancing in a progressive series from mere impressionism up to scientific discrimination. Here, too, it will be convenient to begin with the most primitive in the scale, for it is where the art itself began. " Impressionism " is the significant term by which it is known, since it is based almost wholly on the impressions which a reader obtains in his reading and takes away from it. These are often an indefinite residuum from what has been perused, resulting in a vague sentiment of favour or disfavour toward the book itself. It finds its outlet in commendation of the work to the attention of other readers, or perhaps its condemnation. No distinct reason is given, beyond an impression, pleasing or displeasing, analogous to the good or bad taste which certain foods leave. The reason for such a flavour it may be as difficult to give in one case as in the other. Probably if the reader were driven to the wall for an answer to the question, Why do you not like this book ? he could not frame a reply that would satisfy his own sense of justice to the author. It is like the injustice of impressions which follow the first meeting with certain strangers. They may be very worthy people, but the impression they make is as unfavourable as it is unwarranted. Later it passes away, and possibly is succeeded by the other extreme.

*Impression-
iam the
earliest form
of criticism
to the
individual.*

This is not so often the case with books, since they reveal all their character at once, if they are written with the clearness they ought to have as the first quality of their composition. Accordingly the first impressions of a literary work are usually apt to be lasting. They are also commonly considered a sufficient basis for that judgment which rests upon impressions alone.

Books usually reveal their character at once.

The value of these it is possible both to overrate and to underrate, depending as they do largely upon the intuitive discrimination of the reader. As there are persons in social and civil affairs whose opinions, though formed with rapidity, can be accepted with certainty, so the judgment of some readers can be taken on the ground of their first impressions. Their literary sense is a gift, their good taste an endowment as distinguished from high cultivation, which, however, is not looked for in the ordinary reader. Neither is it to be considered here what such an one might become if the natural gift were improved by cultivation. On the other hand, the impressions of one not having this native insight may be worth comparatively little. His sensations on rising from the perusal of a book may be as untrustworthy for

The value of impressions variable.

another's guidance as if he were colour-blind. His cold blue might be in reality warm red to other eyes, his dazzling yellow a restful green. To this proverbial uncertainty of individual opinion may be added the misfortune of a personal obliquity in the mental vision. The witness may have a defective eyesight that would debar his testimony in the courts, and the friend upon whom another relies for advice and direction in reading may be no more worthy of trust than a colour-blind connoisseur in an art gallery, or a near-sighted companion in the street. As a single kind of criticism, then, impressionism is not equivalent to infallibility. It may approach truth and justice, but it is just as likely to be far removed from them. Whatever it does is by instinct rather than by training; and sometimes it runs back on the trail instead of the way the quarry has gone.

Nevertheless a great deal has been said in defence of impressionism as a basis of criticism. Some have gone so far as to assert that "criticism is the critic,"[1] and that all that can be demanded of him is that he "come to his subject with an open mind."[2] In the same spirit it has been asserted of the dramatic critic, that "the best the reviewer of plays can do is to record the

Impressions as a basis of criticism.

[1] Henry James.   [2] John Burroughs.

impressions made by any performance upon his own mind, which should be, however, as sensitive as the film of a camera."[1]   Still another concludes that, " after all, the test of utterance is, How does it affect us ? This is the absolute treatment of literature, that is, the natural treatment."[2]   By these and others, the doctrine is distinctly stated that personal impressions must be for each one the criteria by which he is to judge of literary achievements. As contrasted with the methods which were in vogue in the last century there is certainly a wide departure from them. The laws and principles which were partly laid down in critical literature, or which, more conveniently, were supposed to be codified in the critic's brain, are shelved by this impressionistic rule, which recommends " lending one's self confidingly to the author, and taking passively and gratefully the mood and images he suggests."

This impressible mood has its advantages, and even its necessity, if the mind of the reader is to be the final arbiter. The guest whose character is to be estimated should by all means be cordially received and given the freedom of the house. No prepossessions should be harboured which will interfere with just apprehension and

The impressible mood of the reader's remind.

---

[1] *The Forum.*   [2] Gates's *Essays of Jeffrey*, xii.

fair judgment. The mind of the reader in like manner will be as wax under the impress of the author's signet. He will give him a fair chance to lodge his sentiments in the reader's understanding. After he is clearly understood, judgment may follow.

Much, however, depends upon clear understanding in determining the value of personal criticism. If Maginn's maxim, repeated by Sydney Smith, is followed, " not to read a book too carefully lest the reviewer be prejudiced by it," and thus be warped from his preconceptions, then the verdict pronounced will have a corresponding value. It will be the verdict of prejudgment, founded, perhaps, on a personal grudge, certainly on ignorance. On the other hand, if the mind be unprejudiced, and the apprehension of the author's meaning clear and definite, the impression is of the first consequence to the critic. He must begin to base his estimates upon it. He cannot base them honestly upon another man's impression. If the sky is grey to him, he need not say that it is blue because Ruskin tells him that he has no eye for colour. His reply will be, " It so impresses me ; and I have the same right to my impressions that every man has." So far the ground he stands upon is incontestable. Aristotle, Sainte-

Beuve, and Arnold rest their judgments each upon his own impressions. " Man is the measure of all truth unto *himself*," as some one sagely says; but in saying it the last word should have been emphasised, if it was not. He is not necessarily the measure of it to others.

It is at this point that the limits of the impressionist method begin to appear. It is a useful and true method for the critical reader's own understanding, but not of necessity for the minds of other men. The personal rule is universal only in the sense that each reader may adopt it for himself. Its conclusions cannot be forced upon another. If bitter ale has a relish for Jones, no one must deny that it impresses him agreeably; but it must not therefore be concluded that Adams should be similarly impressed. He has an equal propensity for being favourably impressed with water, while Johns may have a taste for Burgundy that the other two cannot appreciate from entirely opposite points. It is the same with books and readers in different departments of literature and in different classes in the same department. One may have the relish for Fielding that will carry him through the ruts and over the hills with *Tom Jones;* and he can find eminent authori-

The restrictions of Impressionism.

ties who have pronounced it a fine excursion in English fiction of the eighteenth century. Another will delight as much in the refinements of George Eliot's psychological introspections; and a third may prefer Hawthorne's mystic undercurrents moving with the remorselessness of tidal law and fate. Each one may revile the other for his strange liking, but each has only to remember that his own '' impression '' is subject to the same reviling.

This limitation of impressionism qualifies it as a working method. It is right and proper and good enough for one person; but whether it is effective and trustworthy for any other person, and for hundreds of others, depends entirely upon certain qualities in the critic which are far beyond his mere capacity of receiving impressions. These must be of the right kind and not merely powerful. It is not enough for a man to believe what he likes is good. He must know that it is good independent of his personal liking—or disliking, for that matter. So the difference in impression which the same book makes on different minds should give something of uncertainty to the value of individual impression as a final arbiter of good and evil, right and wrong in literary performances. One man's food is another's poison even where the taste of both is normal and healthy. Is there anything radically wrong in the system of him who cannot approach poison ivy ? or radically right in him who can handle it with impunity ? The answer is that it is not good for most people, nor good to experiment upon.

Then, too, the worst of it is, that impressions are so subject to change with advancing years and altered conditions. What adult is there who does not smile over the ideals and idols of his youth ? How even on different days and in different moods present worship of present literary heroes varies. A bright sky and good news make *Butler's Analogy* almost entertaining; while mist, mud, and no mail will render a boy unimpressible to the charms of *Robinson Crusoe* and a man to those of the *Complete Angler*, *Pepys's Diary*, *Boswell's Johnson*, or *Noctes Ambrosianæ*.

Let impressionism, then, stand for what it is worth—the foundation of all honest judgment, but nothing more. As in the foundation of buildings, it is usually of the same character in all—the common stone of the neighbourhood, so in reading impressions are the common beginnings of judgment. What is built upon this foundation may differ as the hut of the primeval savage and the mansion of wealth or the temple of learning. The hut may do for the primitive man, but in nothing would his primitiveness be more apparent than in calling it a villa, a library, or a cathedral.

In the practical work of reviewing, also, impressions are to be taken at their values. These are as diverse, variable, fickle, and fluctuating as the stock market. There are investments which are always above par, and criticisms which can always be counted on. There are others which, like new financial schemes, were brilliant yesterday and to-day are flat. Sometimes boldness passes for brilliancy. As Leslie Stephen remarks: " A clever man has turned over the last new book of travels or poetry, and has given us his first ' impressions ' with an audacity which almost charms one by its extraordinary naïveté." If now this brave would confine himself to the bounds set by such advocates of impressionism as Lemaître and Anatole France, according to whom " the critic can hope only to express his own tastes, preferences, and impressions, *without pronouncing judgment*," then little harm would be done, since his impressions might easily be distinguished from his judgments, if the latter were carefully kept to himself. Meantime it is possible for even the critic himself to come to a distrust of his own vivid first impressions after they begin to fade and give place to sober reflection. The pyrotechnic impressions of the spectacular drama in its midnight *finale* have mostly vanished by the next high-noon, and the playgoer wonders in what unreal world he was living twelve hours before. He will sometimes have the same dazed feeling on laying down a novel, especially if it be far along in the night. The next day he will tear up his written " impressions," and recall the proverb about the untrustworthiness of early ones — too early perhaps.

As has been intimated, it is for the personal and primary stage of criticism that the impressionistic method is chiefly valuable to the beginner. The veteran's first impressions are sometimes as true as his conclusions; but so keen a critic as Professor Saintsbury does not hesitate to publish his charming Essays on Victorian Writers under the title of *Corrected Impressions.* How many reviewers might be glad to give revisions of their early or hasty work under a similar caption. Advancing years, larger knowledge, wider experience, and more sense, have frequently readjusted the impressions of their earlier or busier days, and

Impressionism belongs chiefly to the primary stages of criticism.

have also enabled them to receive impressions that can be trusted to coincide with subsequent conclusions. It is, after all, the adept who has arrived at the enviable stage where intuition and experience meet, who is the devoted champion of the impressionistic method. Beginners are safer in trusting the impressions of such rather than their own. And yet they should learn how to be impressed.

If they could do this by following directions, the first one should be: " For the time surrender yourself to the author without reserve." Believe in him as if he were an oracle. Accept what he *The first condition of true impression.* says for all the meaning and worth his words will carry, with the constant thought that possibly what he says may have reasons beyond present investigation and attainment. If, instead, one goes along with him disputing every step, opposing every statement, denying every conclusion, the impressions he makes will be as few and feeble as those of light and sunshine upon one who is out of sorts with himself and ready to quarrel with everybody else. If such an one should condescend to examine the sun critically, the only impression he would get would be of the spots on it, and would therefore condemn it as a first-class lighting-plant. There is no bask in such a spirit, no receptivity, and therefore no deep and valuable impressions.   He is a disciple of the blue-glass-solarium theory, and what sunshine he gets is toned with indigo.   Or worse, the medium may be wrinkled, producing grotesque distortions, like the poor window-lights of old houses, which the courts regard as invalidating the testimony of eye-witnesses looking through them.

A passive mood toward the author for the time, then, is the first condition of being impressed by him.   It does not follow that the impression must be favourable; only that it be a true copy, and not marred by preconceptions and oppositions.   What shall be done with the impression is another question and a later process; but at first one has no more call to resist the words he is reading than the paper has to resist the type—if accurate impression be the first condition of all criticism.

VII

CENSORIOUSNESS

"This trade of calumny was in vogue fifty years ago; in fifty more it will probably have altogether ceased."—TAINE.

IMPRESSIONISM receives the stamp of an author's ideas with pleasure or otherwise. It may be to the reader like the pressure of a friendly hand, or like the grip of a steel gauntlet. In either case it is an impress upon the receptive faculty, and a prior process to the revelation of the impression in its own kind of criticism. It is largely a condition of passivity.

Activity is a prevailing condition of the next species of criticism—censoriousness,—a kind which in an ascending ethical scale should not rank above the lowest. Being active, its logical order places it second. Moreover, its near kin-ship to adverse criticism of one person by another makes it so easy and common in literature that it should receive early and strict attention.   Like the troublesome element in a public assembly, it must receive more attention than it deserves before business can proceed. It would be pleasanter to dismiss it with a word or two, and pass to more agreeable branches of the general subject; but it is itself a thing of so many disagreeable words that it has forced itself into notice, particularly in times past, and at the present time in places where ancient traditions survive. It must be admitted, however, that in a modified form there are occasions when it has a value, and becomes a necessary and useful quality in the judgment of some kinds of literature.

Notably it is the easiest and cheapest form of active criticism.   No great effort or acumen A cheap form is required to discover imperfections of criticism. in most mundane things of man's doing and making.   It is so much easier, moreover, to find the flaw than not to make one, and to detect it in the work of someone else than to avoid it in one's own.   For these reasons there is no end of the criticism which points out nothing but faults, or such excellences as seem disfigurements in the eyes of the self-constituted censor.   Much of such criticism is due to an imperfectly developed understanding and to tastes that are unformed.   More is due to a disposition to be severe, and more still to a fear that unless this censorious air is assumed the critic will be regarded as lacking in perception. Most often it is taken on to cover the disability to exercise the higher art of discovering excellences. Occasionally, too, it must be conceded in charity, such flippant censoriousness proceeds from an attack of physical or mental indigestion. Nothing else can explain certain so-called critical performances which are distinguished for absence of knowledge, sound sense, and good nature. No doubt this is a malady to which all writers are subject at times; but no field for its vagaries is so inviting as that of criticism. The object of attack is close at hand, the vulnerable points are the apparent ones, and the pen is sharp, and the critic himself is generally safe behind the screen of his anonymity. Furthermore, the object of attack has no chance to defend himself. Often the ambushed foe is not worthy of the author's steel; but if he were, the hedge belongs to the porcupine, and the few who have turned aside from the highway of letters to combat fretful quills have found that this kind of warfare is to the advantage of the occupant of the hedge. Accordingly many misstatements are allowed to go uncorrected, and more misjudgments, blunders of ignorance, and

7

wilful misrepresentations to remain unnoticed. To correct them, if worth the while, would only provoke a fresh attack with similar result. Determined censoriousness is beyond conviction of anything except its own necessity of being a censor, in order to make good its assumption of critical acumen.

It should be said to the credit of a progressive art, that the parading of an author's literary defects does not constitute the stock employment of the ablest critics as it formerly did.   No Jeffrey can long succeed in our time in starting a conspiracy to dethrone a Wordsworth.   Dr. Johnson's trampling on Gray cannot be imitated without something of the sort in return.   Keats could not be killed by a syndicate of reviewers in the last decade of this century, and Scott would fare far better at its end than he did at its beginning.   The humane spirit which prevails in modern warfare has at last crept into criticism. Savage weapons of ridicule and satire, sarcasm and billingsgate have been cast aside for childish critics to soldier with.   If writers must still be done to death, it is with the rapier rather than the bludgeon.   If they must be dissected alive, soothing and sometimes soporific anæsthetics are administered generously. Often indeed the subject is injured more by the chloroform than by the knife; but a considerate spirit is manifested. Vivisection is bad enough in skilled hands, but when it gets into the heads and hearts of youth and inexperience in literary judgment repressive admonition is in order, and the recommendation to leave this sort of censorship to their seniors.

The elders whose tradition has survived in musty reviews were famous in this surgical business. As with their contemporaries in medicine, what the knife and the saw began the red-hot iron completed, to the satisfaction of the performer, if not of the patient. Usually, " it was a famous victory " like the battle of Blenheim to the ancient trooper, and was accomplished by similar methods and with corresponding results. A few examples taken from the literary history of this Tartar period may be interesting, even if they bring no instruction that is needed by the present generation of reviewers.

Examples of
censorious
criticism in
the past.

It is not necessary to decide the question as to whether it was criticism or consumption that killed Keats. The first doubtless hastened the second. Byron and Shelley believed that an article in the *Quarterly Review* on his " Endymion " was the finishing stroke. It might have deeply wounded a less sensitive man. In sub-

stance the writer of it, said to be Croker, remarked, that he had

" made superhuman efforts to get beyond the first
four books without becoming any better acquainted
with their meaning than with that of the three
books which he had not looked into ; that while the
author has powers of language, rays of fancy, and
gleams of genius he belongs to Leigh Hunt's school
of poetry." (Hunt was a Whig, the *Quarterly*,
Tory.) " This author is a copyist of Mr. Hunt,
but ten times more tiresome than his prototype ;
his nonsense is gratuitous, he writes it for its own
sake, and more than rivals the insanity of his master. He writes at random the suggestions of his
rhyme without having hardly a complete couplet to
endorse a complete idea in the book. If any one
should be bold enough to purchase it, and patient
enough to get beyond the first book and find any
meaning, we entreat him to make us acquainted
with his success ; we shall then return to the task
which we now abandon in despair."

Those who have read " Endymion " before
reading this estimate will regard it as a revelation — of undiluted spleen. *Blackwood* was
even more abusive, telling the poet to go back
to his gallipots, it being a wiser and better
thing to be a starved apothecary than a starved
poet. If they did not kill him they prevented

the completion of " Hyperion "—the fragment
which Byron pronounced to be " as sublime as
Æschylus."

Other instances might be narrated at length
with quotations from the literature of the
shambles. Names only can be en- *The effect
upon authors.*
umerated to direct further investigation by those who may be curious in such
matters. Shelley's critics succeeded in driving
him into exile with the confession : " My faculties are shaken to atoms and torpid; I can
write nothing, for it is impossible to compose
except under the assurance of finding sympathy in what you write." Moore and Byron
were attacked with similar scurrility, but the
one having Irish blood, and the other a title,
managed to survive the onslaughts of Jeffrey
and Brougham; by means of a challenge to a
duel in the first instance, and a satirical retort
in the second. Brougham had characterised
Byron's poetry as " effusions spread over a
dead flat, and so much stagnant water," and
adding that he was " an intruder into the
groves of Parnassus," he counselled him " to
forthwith abandon poetry and turn his talents
to better account." Twelve years after, Byron
recalled the " rage, resistance, and redress but
not despondency and despair " which this critique excited in him, inspiring the lines to

" English Bards and Scotch Reviewers," in which he

" Learned to deride the critic's starch decree,
And break him on the wheel he meant for me."

It should be added to Jeffrey's credit that he had the fairness to retract later, and to mourn at Byron's death.

In those warlike days critics were not particular in their choice of weapons. Personalities, slander, sometimes just outside the borders of libel, and often within, were mingled with severity, vulgarity, and abuse in criticism. Ritson, antiquarian, vegetarian, and annotator of English verse, was driven mad by reviewers, who in the shape of assassins appeared to surround his death-bed. It is recorded that Newton abandoned the publication of his " Treatise on Optics " on account of severe premature objections against it which appeared after it was ready for the press. He considered freedom from censorious criticism of greater value than the celebrity his work might bring him; as Racine before him had remarked, that " one criticism had caused him more vexation than the greatest applauses had afforded him pleasure."

A larger movement in hostile criticism was that against the so-called Lake School of poets by the British reviewers,—a phase of the national opposition to principles and tendencies developed by the French Revolution. It took on the violently personal aspect toward the pioneers of a noble verse. "The *Quarterly* reviled, the *Edinburgh* sneered at, and *Blackwood* bullied," Englishmen then as they did Americans at a later day. Jeffrey, with judicial swagger, following the safest current of opinion, did his little best to annihilate one singer after another in the morning of the present century,'—with what partial success may be guessed from testimony which escaped the poets themselves. Coleridge complains that he was forced to abide the brunt of abuse for faults directly opposite. It is pitiful to observe how he tries to account for the malignity of his critics in the *Biographia Literaria*. In his generosity he cannot attribute it to their vindictiveness, envy, or personal dislike. At last he is forced to conclude that it springs from intimacy with Wordsworth and Southey! The malignity which followed the publication of "Christabel" disgusts and disheartens him, since the poem, which had been much admired before it was printed, had afterward met with nothing but abuse. It was *Blackwood's* review of the *Biographia* which "stung him as the other reviews had not, re-

[Side note: Hostility toward the Lake Poets.]

---

¹ Principal Shairp, *Aspects of Poetry*, p. 113.

newing as it did the old anti-Jacobin charge of abandoning his wife and children."

In Wordsworth's instance there is little doubt that his treatment at the hands of the reviewers had a depressing effect on his poetical powers, and notwithstanding the brave fight he made to hold on his course undisturbed, they were prematurely deadened.

Southey appears to have been the bravest of that company. He had a sense of the worth of his work that no adverse criticism could impair for him. He strode on unmindful of the barking at his heels. Not until one Bill Smith called him a renegade did he turn aside, and then only long enough to leave his mark on his assailant. In fact he sometimes employed harsh methods himself, with or without sufficient provocation.

It may be said that authors should not be so sensitive; but it is probable that they have as little responsibility for their proverbial thinness of skin as for the qualities that have made them worth reading. Even critics themselves have been known to have sensibilities when subjected to their own methods of treatment, especially when they ran foul of one another in the good old days of the cane, horsewhip, and pistol,—the days of Berkely and Fraser, of Wolcot and Gifford, of Moore and Maginn. There is an interesting period in the history of criticism to which the quarrels of the British Reviews, Whig and Tory, contribute an abundance of spiteful material, and reveal an amount of sensitiveness unsurpassed by that of any school of poets, essayists, or novelists. There is considerable evidence that authors are not the only class of writers possessing inconvenient sensibilities. These appear to be a race-characteristic, accompanying intellectual development. Europeans do not belong to the pachyderm family and authors have not been providentially provided with rhinoceros hides, as they should have been. The other recommendation, that they go into the book-market with their eyes open to the gauntlet they must run, has more sense in it; and there is still more in the rejoinder of Bentley to a critic who threatened him: " No man was ever written down but by himself." Of one thing the author may be sure, that if he gets blame from one pen he will get praise from another in these days when there are so many doctors to disagree. He may be certain also that if some reviewers speak of his work with favour, others will suddenly have an unconscious bias in the opposite direction. Such is the curious Whig-and-Tory perversity of human nature.

It is to be feared that there is still abroad a criticism which has a theory to serve, a school of writing to encourage, a province to favour, and also, by consequence, which has to demolish the opposites of all these and their advocates and supporters. The bullying tyranny of the swashbuckler age has passed away, to be sure, and critics no longer ride all night in a storm to find an unsavoury fact, but smartness is at a premium, and costs less than antique and bellicose malignity. As Mr. Midhurst remarks in *Friends in Council*, " A large part of hostile criticism is but jubilant flippancy," whose arrogance, as another suggests, " is equalled only by its ignorance." Seriousness there was in the olden time, of a desperate character no doubt, but it had a definite aim and purpose, which modern pertness, voluble and conceited, appears to lack. This offshoot of a superficial, because multifarious, culture is equal to many things rather than much ; and unless division of labour among specialists enter into criticism, damage is likely to be done by the crass innocent who " did n't know it was loaded." It is to the credit of Lowell that he wrote : " Quite as much cruelty of criticism is due to want of thought as to deliberate injustice." Still, we all know the value of the boy's excuse who

" did n't think "; and remember what the master used to do to strengthen his cogitative faculty. Authors do not take this business into their own hands now as they did in Byron's time. Accordingly the incipient reviewer gets reckless in the use of firearms.

Beyond this heedless flippancy one should be as slow to impute graver charges as Coleridge was. Nothing more offensive than prejudice for one school, university, profession, section of the country or world can be supposed to influence criticism in this cosmopolitan age. Some heart may know its own bitterness, but unless it is shown too plainly no one will make the imputation of evil intent with malice aforethought. None but a small-minded critic will be actuated by the petty considerations above mentioned. Therefore the elements of envy and jealousy are to be counted out of respectable criticism in this age when "tomahawk and scalping-knife surgery " has been left to an occasional brave figuring in the feathers and war paint that lent local colour to the times of James Fenimore Cooper and his reviewers.

If, however, a writer is hit by a flying hatchet, instead of throwing it back he will better console himself with this bit of philosophy from Matthew Arnold: " Why should this savage criticism vex me ? You see one's friends enjoy these things so much." The bad feature of this glee on the part of spectators is the effect it has on the public literary conscience, and moral conscience likewise. By and by it becomes analogous to the hardening process attendant upon first tolerating and then enjoying any injury inflicted. It is a question whether the bear family or the English nation suffered the most damage by the noble sport of bear-baiting; and so of the Romans and their gladiatorial contests, and of the Spaniards and Mexicans and their bull-fights. In like manner the baiting of authors by literary bullies did not improve the ethical or critical sensibilities of our fathers in the first quarter of the present century. The same law of reflex retribution is still in force. The man who laughs at injustice has rendered his sense of it a little less keen. While he is admiring the fling of a boomerang at the victim it returns upon himself. Therefore let the smart reviewer have compassion upon that public in whose behalf he exercises his wits, since he may unconsciously be doing them as much harm as the amusement he affords them is great.

Moreover, it is due authors to remember that they generally work in serious moods, with

The comfort afforded others by harsh criticism.

definite purposes, and some painstaking in the investigation of facts. If they need to be brought to book, the same spirit on the part of their critics and an equal equipment of knowledge will serve the interests of literature far better than ignorant, impertinent, and superficial flippancy. The calumny that used to delight our forefathers is a weapon which betrays its own antiquity; and he would now be bold who should risk its blunderbuss recoil. The broadsword of the Lowlander's slashing criticism is equally antique, dangerous, and unfashionable from the rust it has accumulated. It can be found for the most part only in curiosity shops. Both these methods, however, required brain and brawn in handling, which is more than can be said of the empty impudence which is the principal ingredient in later censoriousness.

In accordance with the purpose of these chapters a few practical suggestions should be given at the end of this one in regard to carrying out in practice the principles that have been mentioned. Not that they are by any means approved, or that there is great need of instructing beginners in the art of the fault-finder. A few hints may, however, serve a better purpose not alien to the general design.

One way to make the most capital out of a little is to search for some slight error of statement, due originally, perhaps, to the authority from which it was derived, Inaccuracies. for the sources of history have been known to differ. In the lack of anything better an incorrect date will answer the purpose, since dates are seldom known to vary—after they are once determined by competent authority. One variation from a settled fact or date is sufficient to prove the general carelessness and untrustworthiness of an author, and he may be treated with a disquisition upon inaccuracy or dismissed with supercilious and well merited scorn. Besides, this will afford an excellent opportunity for the reviewer to show that his sources of information are better and his knowledge more accurate, or possibly that he has had access to the latest edition of the *Chronic Cyclopedia.*

Another method of censure is to take a book to task because it differs from the critic's private and personal theories of the subject Disagreement in opinion. in hand, be it religious or political, scientific or literary. There is nothing easier than to condemn departures from one's own views on the first two of the above lines of conviction, and not very difficult to get dogmatic about the last two. It is equally easy to imagine one's own position to be central and vital, and to make it appear so by the abnormal divergence of the examinee. There is no apparent necessity of asking what the absolute standard of truth is in such a case; for it may not be possible to determine. Moreover, if the critic is a law unto himself, why should he not be to a less enlightened person as well? Is he not the appointed corrector of all errors of fact and opinion?

After this there is but one step further that he can go. Motives of the author are the final challenge to his shrewdness and acumen. It may be a little unsafe to pronounce upon them, but the field is a tempting one for exploration and surmise. Once hit upon they are the key to the situation, and explain everything not otherwise to be accounted for. *Imputation of motives.*

It is to be hoped that these methods will not be adopted. They have not the merit of original discovery, since they used to be very common. If they were not too often illustrated now in the cheaper kinds of criticism it might be better to pass them by unmentioned. Possibly the mention of them, without recommendation, is a good way to ensure their avoidance.

VIII

COMMENDATION

" *The Shepherd.* Gude safe us !—that 's grand—and it 's
better than grand, it 's true. I forgie the lads a' their sins,
for the sake o' their free, outspoken praise, when they do
mean to do a kind thing. They lauch far ower muckle at me
in their Magazine ; but I canna deny, I proudly declare 't,
that none o' a' the critics o' this age hae had sic an insight
into my poetical genius, or roused me wi' sic fearsome eloquence. When they eulogise me in that gate, my blood gangs
up like spirits o' wine, and I fin' myself a' gruin' wi' a sort o'
courageous sense o' power, as if I could do ony thing, write a
better poem than the Lay of the Last Minstrel, fecht Bona-
parte gin he was leevin', and snap my fingers in the very face
o' ' The Gude Man.' "

Noctes Ambrosianæ.

D IAMETRICALLY opposed to general
fault-finding is the general praise which
it may be equally easy to bestow when no
**Praise from
a fellow-
craftsman.** hindrances are presented in the form
of a grudging spirit or envious re-
serve. Such generosity is admira-
ble as a testimony to the graciousness of the

critic whatever his vocation may be, but when it is exhibited by one whose labours lie in the same sphere as the author's it becomes doubly considerate. At the same time there is always an opportunity for the best appreciation by a fellow-craftsman, since he can understand better than a layman the difficulties besetting work in his own line. The sympathetic factor in judgment will in such an one be raised to the highest power. He will be full of charity because full of knowledge. This is what an author might reasonably expect when he falls into the hands of a member of his own guild, as he frequently does under the modern custom of sending books to specialists to be reviewed. How far the theory corresponds with actual practice must be left to the opinion of writers who have been served by their fellows. In this, as in other matters, no doubt, experience will differ with different persons, times, and critics.

Sometimes kindly criticism proceeds from other motives. As censoriousness may spring from personal dislike, unwarrantable and unjust, so praise may flow from From friends. strong liking for a book or its author. To such a sentiment the friendly reviewer has as good a right as the censor has to its opposite. Moreover, in the open court of public sentiment it is probable that those who err on the side of charity will fare as well as those whose ink is too full of the gall of bitterness. The world is complacent toward a lover in literature as in life, in spite of Pope's lines to a critic. On the other hand, extreme laudation, like severe censure, is apt to go for nothing, when its source is expected to be friendly to the author.

Thus far has been borne in mind that work only which is over-praised. It must not be **Deserving** forgotten that there may be such as **work.** shall deserve all the commendation that even a friend can bestow. Everyone can specify examples of literature whose excellence in one department or another is equal to the highest opinion that contemporary friendship can form of it. Our great English authors have had their appreciative admirers in their own time, beginning with Shakespeare, notwithstanding all that has been written about tardy recognition. Yet what one of these admirers has done more than justice to Shakespeare and Milton, to Bacon and Newton, to Scott and Thackeray ? Enough has been written in qualification and detraction concerning all of them, and no praise that they have ever received from devoted followers has offset blame from foes. Occasionally, therefore, almost unstinted laudation may be no more than an author deserves from any critic, and from his friends as a matter of course.

In general, however, it must be added, that this license to extol depends for its warrant upon the eminence of the author. In such acknowledged eminence the inexperienced reviewer sometimes takes refuge. He deems it safe to eulogise him whom the general voice commends. This would be safe if the performance of the best writers were always uniform and equally meritorious; but this cannot be assumed. It is unfortunately not always true that the well that is oftenest drawn upon yields the most abundantly. At least the comparison does not hold with respect to the productive mind. There must be fresh springs back of the pool, the supply sources must be kept full from the waters under the earth or in the sky. In an occasional or eventual failure of such tributaries eminent authors have sometimes done work which is not worthy an earlier reputation, nor up to their highest attainment. Commercial reasons, habit, momentum acquired, and general expectation have kept them at work after the supply of ideas began to fail. There has seemed a sad irony in the title of Dickens's *Great Expectations*. It was too late to meet those of a delighted public. Scott would have laid down his pen when it began to run dry if it had not been for the debt of honour, and many a writer has not known when his best work was done. For this reason the critic is not always warranted in repeating the old praise with the appearance of a new book by an eminent author.

So likewise there may occur seasons of drouth in his best years followed by a corresponding variation in the product. Such a year of scarcity is very likely to be the precursor of a prolific season, as in nature the fallow field and the off-year favour a succeeding abundance. But it is the business of the critic to know what the harvest is in any year. He is not to mistake the last season's report of any bureau for this year's. Many readers will get the start of him if he does. The general sense, which is very near the best judgment of the adept, will reverse his sentence if he does not anticipate its verdict. Accordingly he will be on the look-out for variations in the literary output of any authors whose reputations may seem to warrant continuous commendation. The best of them, like the first of them, will nod at times, with the rest of animate creation. The law of uniformity is always conditioned by the law of variety. And the study of variation and its causes is one of the most interesting and profitable in the realm of criticism.

Some of these causes are deserving of critical censure. When an author is trading on his reputation, whether at the so- licitation of publishers or the public, it is the privilege of the literary censor to call attention to the evidences. Respectable manufactories have a label for inferior goods which gives no clue of relationship to the first-class fabrics that bear the trade-mark of the firm. Unfortunately, the author has no corresponding device, unless it be an anonymous name, which would have no value in the book-market. It is his own signature that sells the book, and sometimes a book that is not up to the standard expected from the trade-mark displayed. The wares that have been foisted upon the market in this way constitute a curious chapter in the commerce of literature. Fables and sermons, wonder-books and histories have been driven to the stalls, shepherded by notable names. The quality has usually been in an inverse ratio to the quantity, as is apt to be the case in all over-production. Signs of such over-production it is the critic's right to discover and publish. At least he need not make his note of approbation so loud as is the popular call for fresh instalments from an exhausted fund of fact or fiction, pleasing verse or sparkling prose. On the other hand, when a superior writer is doing good work, especially if he be a master workman, he has earned all the appreciation that a critic can conscientiously bestow. The best craftsmen most need encouragement, for they are often soonest discouraged; being usually noted for self-depreciation, and severe criticism of their own work. Moreover, the best productions are most needed. The poor, in literature as in life, are always with us. They need no premiums offered for their multiplication. Like weeds they require no culture, and to thin them out some hold to be the chief end of criticism.

In his approbation the critic will take into account the promise of youthful and inexperienced *Encouragement of promising writers.* enced writers if, like Sainte-Beuve, he should happen to have a quick discernment of nascent genius. He will thus imitate the hospitality of successful authors, who as a rule have been helpful to young writers of promise. An encouragement that is not necessarily patronage will find its place among the qualifications for the criticism which is most serviceable to letters. On the other hand, perhaps the law of the survival of the fittest demands repressive measures in judgment, lest the land be overrun with mediocrity and overwhelmed by a yellow flood.

From time to time a voice may be heard in the wilderness of criticism crying out against all praise of authorship. As long ago as Coleridge it complained that " the eulogies of critics without taste or judgment are the natural reward of authors without feeling or genius." This sentiment has been re-echoed in many forms and places, the commonest version being that which states or implies a bargain of some sort between author and reviewer worthy of being ranked with a political deal. Epithets are freely applied, such as log-rolling, wire-pulling, and the terminology of mutual-admiration societies is largely drawn upon to make all friendly recognition appear like a commercial transaction. Of course the element of acquaintance and friendship is detrimental to ideal judgment in the abstract; that is, if the author, according to the tenor of a law not so very ancient, is presumed to be a criminal until he is proved to be innocent. The accused, fortunately, in these more enlightened days has the benefit of a reversal of this supposition. He has friends to speak a good word for him, and counsel assigned who may help create a public sentiment in his favour, assisted so generously by the press that it is sometimes difficult to get twelve jurymen whose opinion has not been influenced by their newspapers. Much care is also taken to favour the defendant in many ways during the trial itself, until, in one way and another, he becomes a person almost as privileged as an American tenant. But the writer of books should not be thus privileged; nor should he have friends to speak a kindly word out of their intimate knowledge of his personality; for has he not tossed a book into the market-place as an anarchist might throw a bomb and defy the multitude to pick it up ? It matters not if the book be harmless, wholesome, or useful, it is to be treated as an explosive until a self-constituted court of high crimes and misdemeanours shall pronounce that it is not dangerous, or possibly that it is a godsend. Meantime any suggestion from those who might have said as much in advance is considered as premature and biassed testimony. Moreover this might be open to the suspicion of being paid for in some coin or other. Now, what if all this should be granted, would the author thus favoured by his friends be any better or worse off than the ordinary man who goes in and out among his fellow-men, who are his friends or his enemies in various degree ? Is he likely to get less justice in the average estimate because his friends are cordial in their commendation; or more justice because his foes are just as hearty in their censure ? Should the formation of sentiment about each member of society be left to a volunteer committee qualified to speak about persons by their love of speaking or writing, and by having free access to printing-presses ?—to which might be added a greater or less reputation in judging of character. Possibly such a committee might themselves at times be glad of the kindly partiality of friends, lest their enemies should have a monopoly in creating a counter current of opinion regarding their fitness for such assumed responsibilities. Such is the case in a measure between authors and reviewers. The maxim of the latter is, or used to be before Taine, that the author is to be judged by his work alone. A later maxim equally valuable is, that a book should be estimated by such aids as an acquaintance with the writer's surroundings, qualifications, and purposes can supply. These are elements in the calculation which friends can furnish, while strangers cannot, and the indifferent and the ill-disposed will not.

In the editing of an author's works by another person, which is a sort of interpretative criticism, the more intimate the friend the better will be the interpretation. He can often read a meaning between lines which the stranger is not qualified to discover through lack of acquaintance with a life which it was impossible to incorporate in literature. There is so much of it which like vapour escapes the plodding analyst busy with his rules and formulas, his retorts and crucibles of criticism. Is there good reason why a friend should not have a share in administering an author's literary legacies in his lifetime or after his decease, so long as such administration is understood to be an affair of volunteers? At any rate, the partiality of friendship may be admitted as a counter-weight against the prejudice of possible enemies, not to mention the worse element of careless indifference on the part of the unconcerned. If final judgment of literary products comes from the public which reads books and criticisms, it is only fair that one extreme of estimate be offset by another. The friendly critic or the charitable optimist will thus be allowed to sweeten the potion for the public into which the severe pessimist has cast a root of bitterness, or the careless, the essence of flatness.

Friendly criticism counterbalances hostile.

An illustration of this antidotal process is furnished by two critics, supposed often to resemble each other, but whose critical tempers

are antipodal, namely Carlyle and Emerson.
They both saw the good and the bad in whatever they undertook to estimate; but while the
bad emphasised itself to Carlyle the good impressed Emerson more strongly. He was
always on the lookout for something good,
sometimes finding the one good thing in a
work which Carlyle would have sweepingly
condemned because of overbalancing defects.
Even of a noxious weed, Emerson used to say:
" It is a plant whose virtues have not yet been
discovered." The same patient charity was
extended often to indifferent composition.
Montesquieu's did not belong to this class of
writing, but Emerson's note upon that author
may serve as a contrast to Carlyle's strictures
upon another. " There have been," Emerson
writes, " men with deeper insight; but, one
would say, never a man with such abundance
of thought: he is never dull, never insincere,
and has the genius to make the reader care for
all that *he* cares for."

In his diary, November 2, 1831, Carlyle, in
different temper, sets down the following
opinion of Charles Lamb: " I sincerely believe
him to be in some considerable degree insane.
A more pitiful, rickety, gasping, staggering,
stammering fool, I do not know." Lamb's
spontaneous humour strikes him as " a ghastly

make-believe of wit; in fact more like diluted
insanity than anything of real jocosity, humour,
or geniality." After this no one will dispute
Carlyle's right to the title some one has bestowed upon him, " a bundle of sour prejudices "; or to the verdict that " his bad blood
and venom is worse than his bad criticism."
" Bad," no doubt, in the sense of its occasional temper; but when good-tempered there
are qualities in it which are worthy of careful
study, and excellences which give. him an
enviable pre-eminence as a critic. Too often,
however, these have to be extracted from the
prickly burr with the customary exasperation
attendant upon such a process.

It should be understood that criticism by
friends does not necessarily mean blind adulation or servile panegyric. The day
of these things passed away long before that of scathing censure. Laudation without measure belongs to
despotic times and places, and the literature
of this sort of criticism pertains to the ages of
decaying empires, particularly in Latin and
Romance countries. When royal favour or
liberty and life depended upon adulation approaching adoration, and the language of the
West was strained to the extravagance of
orientalism, there were examples of laudatory

comment paralleled only by the condemnatory hyperboles inspired by a British or American sense of independence which followed the outcome of two revolutions. As a rule, flattery is not an outgrowth of independence. Candour, even between friends, is much more germane to the atmosphere of free states. In the republic of letters panegyric is as out of place and out of fashion as to address a magistrate by the Roman title of " Your Eternity," or the oriental " Heaven-Descended-Everlasting-August Ruler of the Universe and Lord of Twenty-four Umbrellas."

The generous commendation of a book by a friendly critic is a far different matter. It is analogous to that which a connoisseur in painting might bestow on such good points as are apparent in the work of a friend. If he charitably overlooks the defects in it and keeps discreet silence, he will no more than compensate for the greater number who will not let the public go unadvised in regard to the existence of faults. He has his place, accordingly, in the world of criticism, even if he speak nothing but smooth things.

So far it has been supposed that he does this and nothing more; but he often does something else of equal value. He points out faults in a more effective manner than the hostile critic, who loses half his usefulness in the acerbity of his method. No great improvement has ever been discovered to follow the ramping and roaring style of reproof. Plenty of strife has been stirred up; but it is not in ordinary human nature for the writer to show that he has followed suggestions that have been shouted to him in public with derision. As on the athletic field there may be a quiet, kindly word of counsel quickly followed, and also loud, censorious coaching that is not obeyed with cheerful alacrity, so in the larger arena of letters the good-natured strictures of a friend are far more productive of amendment than the supercilious or patronising advice of the man who knows it all; not to mention the man who is not quite sure that he does, but has a profound faith in glib generalities as a substitute for knowledge.

Practical directions to the friendly critic are almost as superfluous as to the unfriendly. Each will find his own opportunity of displaying his attitude toward books and their authors. It will do no harm, however, to make suggestions in this direction as in the other.

First of all, the charitably disposed reviewer will avoid the methods of the uncharitable as a matter of course. He will not make accuracy of dates the essence of history, nor his own private opinion the meridian of truth, nor be over-confident in assigning motives. This for the negative side of his virtues. On the positive side there will at least be the opposites of these strictures. He will remember that infallibility is not demanded in human knowledge or memory; that one man's view of what is true or best in religion and politics, in science and literature, may be as correct as another's, conditions being the same; that if the improvement of literature is the highest aim of criticism, it will be accomplished soonest by an optimistic temper and broad-minded judgment. So much being granted as fundamental, there may follow such sympathy with the author's positions as comes from clear understanding of his purpose and from correct interpretation of his meaning, if it is capable of a twofold construction. Such a critic will count it no sin to overlook minor offences, where even great authors are not always without fault; nor will he deem it worse to be civil and gracious in literature than in life, having no call for the bluntest candour or for an eager admonition about trifles that are more creditable in the breach than the observance. These he can safely leave to people who have no reason to

be scrupulous or considerate, and who will see
to it that the balance of praise and blame is at
least equally adjusted.   Which will in the end
do most for the promotion of what is worth
most in literature may be an open question.   If
it were to be decided by a general show of
hands, there is little doubt that the counsels of
the friendly would be approved by the majority
as best serving the interests of letters.

IX

APPRECIATION

" The value of all masterly work in art and science is conditioned by the kinship and capacity of the mind to which it speaks.   It is only such a mind as this that possesses the magic word to stir and call forth the spirits that lie hidden in a great work."—SCHOPENHAUER.

BETWEEN censorious and laudatory criticism there is the usual mean, as between all extremes.   It is characterised by what is good and useful in both praise and blame, dis-**Appreciation** tributed according to the deserts of **defined.**   the performance to be estimated. " Appreciation " expresses, so far as one word can express, the principal features of such criticism.   These are understanding and sympathy.   Underneath the word itself lurks the primitive idea of weighing, as in a balance, with neither fear nor favour, recognising merits, and understanding the difficulties which are in the way of all worthy endeavour and achievement. Still it is judicial in temper, testing products by trustworthy standards, and guided in its decisions by such knowledge as can be obtained to throw light upon the work and its production.

There is, however, an element in appreciative criticism which does not enter into the strictly judicial estimate of literature. Some have considered it opposed to impartial discrimination. This quality may be called by a newly coined name—sympatheticism—denoting the capacity for sympathy with an author, and inclination to it, rather than the actual agreement with him at all times and in all respects. Its opposite is the latent antagonism which is the habitual attitude of much criticism, the spirit which considers every piece of literary composition presumably bad until it has been proved positively good—mediæval justice applied to books and authors. Contrasted with this grim antagonism is the open-mindedness and optimism which is capable of believing that there is something good in every book until the bad has revealed itself or shown its preponderance over the good. Accordingly it may be safely held that a sympathetic spirit is entirely consistent with fair judgment. It is nothing more than the charitable optimism which believes in the better side of humanity rather than the worse, and prefers to call attention to what has been done with a good purpose and with fair results rather than to the inevitable flaws that exist in all mundane achievements. Coleridge has interpreted this sentiment as follows:

" He who tells me there are defects in a new work, tells me nothing which I should not have taken for granted without his information. But he who points out and elucidates the *beauties* of an original work, does indeed give me interesting information such as experience would not have authorised me in anticipating."

Such a temper, let it be repeated, is essential to just appreciation, as its opposite is a barrier to fair estimation of literary values. The judicial criticism into which this open-mindedness does not enter ceases to be judicial. Judgment and discrimination are not essentially narrow and exclusive. The best judgment, on the contrary, is that which is formed on the broadest foundation, and based on the widest assemblage of particulars. No final decision of the courts is made until all the evidence is in. Any exclusion or one-sided view of testimony is fatal to the reputation of the judge. He is constantly widening his observation of facts, weighing their relative value, but hospitable to all.   The critic who does the same will obtain similar advantages.   He will secure large views of the wide reaches of literature which another will fail of who searches only for flaws and defects and faults.   This last process in itself tends to blind the searcher to the higher and nobler qualities of composition, as the sordid hunt for the waste of the streets dulls the sense of grandeur and beauty lying beyond the town in mountain and forest.

It is possible, of course, that defects may assume gigantic proportions and overtop ex-cellences; but, as a rule, such dis-proportion of the bad over the good is confined to those productions which are cheap in every sense. Publishers know their public and what wares will be likely to meet its demands. If the public taste be good the bad in literature will not prevail.   Therefore it should not be sought by the critic nor advertised by his notice of it.   His better business will be to look for the preponderating values which are taken for granted as existing in every respect-able publication.   They are a part of that great body of " the best that is known and thought in the world."   They differ in differ-ent books and times and places, but, taken together, they are the sum of the best thoughts and their expression. In finding this body of the best the critic is following his legitimate vocation in the world of letters—or at least the main part of it. For one defect which he has to point out, there should be, in the book that has fairly accomplished its purpose, a dozen excellences. These he can afford to appreciate according to their respective and relative value.

His ability to appreciate is also as necessary as his willingness to show his appreciation. Such ability depends upon many *Appreciative qualities.* conditions. Some of them run down among the roots of his being, among other primary capacities and tendencies. The appreciative critic, like the true poet, must first of all be born with the essential qualities of perception and recognition. As much as in the poet's instance, is it true that no one ever came to distinction as a critic who had not an inborn sense of comparative values in literature. This is one of the hardest accomplishments to confer by training and education, if there be no capital stock to trade upon. The fact that no college has ventured to add the degree of Doctor in Criticism to the sixty-odd now conferred may be taken as an evidence of the didactic difficulties in this art. Eminence in it is most often a gift, growing by practice rather than cultivated by precepts. Still something can be done by judicious guidance.

What, then, are some of the qualities which contribute to the appreciative talent ? Just here it may be stated that they are not necessarily such as are required to compose the work to be estimated. Many a man can keenly enjoy and accurately value a painting who knows little about the compounding of colours and less about laying them on. These processes make the value, but do not pass judgment upon its degree. That is another direction in which understanding is employed. It is the same in judging of literary performances. The estimating rather than the building faculty is needed ; the skilled surveyor, weigher, and measurer more than the contractor and builder. Each may know something of the other's specialty, but each knows his own better. So the writer may be his own severest critic without being so good a one as his neighbour the reviewer.

As an offset to this it may be said that the critic will gain something in the art of appreciation if he has done some creative work himself, over and above whatever of creation there may be in the best of critical literature. He will at least the better understand some of the difficulties attending this sort of composition. He will know that in proportion as a book is minted directly from an author's brain, by so much does it differ from compilation of facts, dreary as this process may be; or from weaving these records into a continuous web, perplexing as this may become; or deducing conclusions from their composite evidence, difficult as this may prove. Such original composition may be even more of a tax upon mental and neural energy than the estimate of what it is actually worth after all the pains bestowed upon it. The amateur mechanic bestows tiresome hours upon an invention which the practical engineer pronounces of little value almost at a glance. Even great inventors have been known to waste months over a device which the Patent Office examiner could not approve, as also he could not have put it together. If perchance he may ever have tried his hand at invention he will appreciate such features as point toward usefulness and beauty, and are capable of ultimate development. In like manner, the author-critic will be a more appreciative critic for having been an author; as the artist in colour may be a competent connoisseur, with the added knowledge of the practical art. He will at least understand what it costs to produce effects that appear happy accidents to the uninitiated, and may thus be able to reckon them at their cost value if not at their market price. So much, then, for the question, appearing in many forms, as to whether or not the appreciation of a work of art is increased by a technical knowledge of the processes which produce it.

This knowledge of the cost of production may or may not affect the judgment of the critic as to the value of a given product. If he have himself been that sort of a producer, he will generally appreciate the worth of the performance—no prejudices entering in. He will be able to take his place by the side of the author in his workshop. He may say to him:

No man can see all that has gone into this piece of mechanism or creation unless he himself has attempted something like it. It may be worth much or little to the reading world, but I know whether it was done with difficulty or easily, just as well as I know whether it is useful, interesting, entertaining, or the opposite. I must not let my one kind of knowledge interfere with the other in my published estimate, but the former cannot but soften asperities of judgment if the work is fairly done.

Another cardinal qualification for appreciative criticism lies in a broadly instructed taste. Inborn aptitude is the beginning of preëminent attainment in this direction, but it is not the whole of it. The range of literature is too wide for the natural bent of any single critic. Any one department of letters in these productive times *A broadly instructed taste.* is sufficient to tax a genius of acumen and judgment. In history or fiction, in science or poetry, the production is so constant and abundant that no reader can follow, much less estimate, the sum of it. When therefore he attempts anything like discursiveness in these wide fields, he needs a catholic taste sufficiently educated to be somewhat at home with various writers. More than a general knowledge in several departments cannot be expected of an individual critic. But while this may not be of immediate value to him when attempting special criticism in a single department of literature, his sense of its particular value will be increased by some knowledge of other departments, on the principle that the more a person knows of many things the better will be what knowledge he has of any one thing. He will at least be likely to discover the common principles which, like isothermal lines, run through most phenomena, connecting things apparently remote and in different latitudes. The critic, for example, who confines himself to fiction will appreciate an author's plots, incidents, and characters no less for the acquaintance he may have with science and philosophy. Even so material knowledge as that of geography may be useful in so immaterial a study as that of character, where climatic conditions come into the account. The larger criticism of life must enter into any special work that is not mere specialism. And as life is more than letters, the appreciation of it is more than word-weighing and sentence-measuring. It should be broad and catholic in its equipment, inclusive and sympathetic in its application to literature. What Guy de Maupassant says of the culture of the imagination is equally true in criticism: " If you wish to develop imagination, saturate yourself with scientific facts.''

So likewise the larger criticism implies comprehensive views of circles beyond its immediate object of examination. Principal Shairp has designated this as a prominent feature in Coleridge's criticism, '' presupposing as it did profound and comprehensive thought on questions not lying within, but based on wider principles beyond itself. In everything he took up he strove to reach the fundamental, living idea which gave birth to a system and kept it alive.'' [1]

Comprehensiveness of view.

[1] *Studies in Poetry and Philosophy*, p. 156.

To the same purport is the following by a recent writer who says in substance that

" the mere belletrist criticism of belles-lettres tends not only to magnify the importance of such performance, but to misrepresent its literary value, since this value shifts with different development of intelligence. The specialist fails to adapt himself to the general course of things, and loses his importance in not relating himself to the main mental movement. He becomes enamoured of the verbiage of dead drama of ' Elizabethan and Caroline obscurities' whose total value is less than that of the discoveries of scores of workers in physics and biology, history and invention. He thus becomes a kind of Talmudist, living in a world of word-begotten thoughts, and cannot see the wood for the trees."

Such an arraignment of belles-lettres criticism may serve to indicate the retribution which befalls all narrowness in appreciation of whatever sort. A wide culture *Wide culture.* must underlie the judgment that professes to be wide and fair. How otherwise shall the reviewer give due credit to the author who may happen to lead him into by-ways of knowledge of which he knows little or nothing ? He may adroitly pass by such divergencies from the beaten track of information, but in doing so he may miss what is most original and most interesting to a great number of readers. If he should have the temerity to pronounce judgment on points where he is in the dark, a worse calamity might befall him. Every well-furnished critic will accordingly lay the foundation of his appreciation broadly in wide and diversified attainments. Otherwise he will be able to estimate justly the things only that pertain to his own limited specialty. Reviewing the single book, he may be at home in a question of dramatic verbiage and at sea regarding the historical incident which is unfolded. He may detect a false quantity in a verse, but not the doubtful ethics between the lines. He may know that the rhythm lacks a syllable, and not know that the scientific allusion has lost half its pertinency because the theory in the writer's mind is an exploded one.

Should it be asked if special attainments go for nothing in the field of judgment, the reply *Value of* is, that they are most important *specialism.* where and when they are in requisition. If the work to be estimated is along special lines and professional in character, the specialist is the man to judge of its value,—other things favouring his equity in the procedure. But in the ordinary stream of literature that flows to the reviewer's table only a small

fraction can be denominated entirely professional. For such fraction there must be either
special qualification or incompetent judgment.
For the greater remainder the general critic
must provide such estimates as he can furnish
according to the breadth of his culture, the
catholicity of his taste, and the versatility of
his pen.

This last accomplishment deserves more than
passing mention. Useful in every literary occupation, it is essential in any department of journalism, lest the **Versatility.**
daily reading of large constituencies become
monotonously tiresome. While variety may
be difficult to maintain in editorial columns
when one day is like another, the reviewer has
much to help him in the diversity of books
which are laid before him. They come from
all departments of literature and arrive in
curious disorder. A volume of history is followed by a treatise upon chemistry; an astro-
nomical work by a cheap novel. Theology is
crowded by athletics, and physiology by metaphysics, psychology by the drama, and ethics
by poetry; while between and all around an
overflowing flood of fiction is pouring to the
distress and distraction of the critic. Mental
dyspepsia stares him in the face from the stacks
of literary sweetmeats he must sample or worry

down.   The 'ologies afford a little variety with their heaviness, but not much relief.   He can allow himself little time for adjustment of his faculties as he puts aside one book and takes up the next in order.   His perceptive faculty sometimes gets a strain as he passes from darkness to light, from philosophy to the short story.   Yet his reputation or living may depend upon not carrying the impressions of the last volume into his views of the next.   His critical retina must be cleared of the lingering shadow of the object at which he has been gazing; which he can still see when he closes his eyes.   It would be disastrous, for example, if he should have his vision of scientific writing coloured by the glamour of fiction which he has just been reading.   It might be as fatal to his judgment as the tints of evening twilight to an observer trying to ascertain the colour of Saturn's rings.   On the other hand, it would be hardly fair to the novelist whom he is to estimate to approach his work with a trace of the scientific mood engendered by balancing theory with evidence.   Therefore the critic will cultivate somewhat the qualities of the juggler in passing from one act to another with absolute abandonment of each as he drops it for the next.   This is not easy to do at first.   The taster of books, like the taster of teas, will need

some acquired skill not to let the flavour of
that last brew of Bohea affect this present one
of Souchong, and by consequence the value he
sets upon it. What sort of a taste must be
left to the critic who has dipped into a dozen
or twenty books at a single sitting! Some
estimates that appear in print must be accounted for on the supposition that the over-
taxed reviewer has had successive potions to
taste or swallow of theology, law, medicine,
biology, physics, astronomy, navigation, art,
and drama, all diluted more or less with a wash
of fiction, which like the ocean of the ancient
mariner is everywhere, and too often with the
same undrinkable quality. Verily the appreciative critic deserves commiseration rather
than abuse. His lot is harder than the traditional inspector's, although resembling it in the
variety of districts to be looked into on a single
round.

Still such versatility in judging of the merits
of different books upon diverse subjects is not
impossible. Long practice and some special
training do marvels for the diligent worker in
appreciative criticism as in other departments
of literature. Examples of such attainment
are known to those who are acquainted with
contemporary journalism, which both trains
and employs this kind of ability. It is not

much known to general readers, unless they are able to identify initials with names, or to achieve a still more difficult undertaking,— recognise the critic by his literary style. But there are those in the world of journalism who know, and who watch for the best of work: some to be instructed by it, and to catch the trick of it; others to buy it up in the great market of literary labour and enterprise. The appreciative reviewer's specialty, then, is a broad and diversified one. It is a well informed comprehensiveness in knowledge, and a wide versatility in writing, guided by a broadly instructed taste, itself characterised by an open-mindedness which can discern the possibilities of excellence in every department of human learning and exploration, even if it be sometimes beyond the critic's own attainments.

Such an one will find himself not without examples to imitate. There are many sympathetic critics who " praise the good and leave the bad to decay of itself," holding that there can be no true and helpful criticism without sympathy. As one [1] of them remarks: " We see the real Goethe or Arnold only so far as we have that within us which answers to what there is in him. Like responds to like. Criticism is ap-

Examples of appreciative criticism.

[1] John Burroughs.

preciation." Another[1] calls criticism " an indefinite expansion of the appreciative power ";
and still another[2] terms it " the science of consistency in appreciation." It is the lack of this
quality in Jeffrey, namely, sympathetic imagination enough to identify himself with another
and to look at things from his point of view,
that separates him from Coleridge with his
sympathetic and penetrative imagination, and
from Macaulay also, who seized upon the ruling
traits of character and the strong features of
composition by placing himself in the shoes of
the man and at the desk of the author, and
looking at affairs and life as Hampden did, or
at literature as Milton did. He has been living
with them sympathetically. Sometimes, however, his prejudices get the better of his sympathies, as when he could not do Cromwell
justice by reason of his Whig distrust of all
fanaticism. It required Carlyle's sympathy
with religious enthusiasm to do justice to the
commander of the Ironsides. An even more
sympathetic critic was Professor Wilson, the
greatest, according to Peter Bayne, " that ever
used the English language . . . , and the
most capable, through his range of sympathy,
to discover and appreciate excellence." Of a
later critic, Edmund Gosse, it has been aptly

[1] J. Nichol.   [2] J. M. Robertson.

10

said by Leslie Stephen, that " his most marked
quality is a sympathetic appreciation of what
he is interested in and would have others like,
putting himself in the author's place, the first
step in true criticism, impressing the desire to
read the books he criticises." Of our own
Lowell, an English poet-critic [1] speaks in regard
to " his usual habit of establishing intimate
and confidential relations with his author," occasional exceptions being noted. On the
ethical aspects of this topic President Porter
takes the ground that all just criticism must be
generous and genial:

" For its cardinal maxim is, the critic cannot be
just to an author unless he puts himself in the
author's place. Its comprehensive rule is, if you
would understand an author's meaning you must
learn to think as the author thinks, to feel as he
feels, to look at nature and man through his eyes,
to respond to both with his soul, to estimate his
audience as he knew them, to measure the instru-
ments of language and imagery which he had at
command, in their several limitations as well as
their capacities. You must do all these things before you can even begin to judge him. It is only
by seeking fairly and fully to understand a writer
that we are able to enter fully into his feelings, to
catch his spirit, and to estimate his reasonings,

[1] William Watson.

even if we are not convinced of their conclusive-
ness. This criticism wakens enthusiasm, teaches
us to look for excellences rather than search for
defects, prompts unreserved enjoyment and generous delight in beauties revealed, bids the reader
be lenient to inadvertences and defects in a writer
of positive merit, because it teaches him how they
are to be accounted for.''[1]

Let this citation stand for any direction the
inexperienced may need in the practice of appreciative criticism. Meantime he may recall
the title which an eminent critic[2] has chosen
to give to a volume of his essays, namely, *Appreciations*, as another,[3] already mentioned, has
called his, *Impressions*. Zola had the honesty
to name his unfavourable ones, *My Hatreds*.
Following the modesty of the first two distinguished critics, the amateur will find his safest
and best course lying in the two directions of
impression and appreciation. Silence is the
best treatment of his hatreds, at least until he
attains the celebrity of Zola.

[1] *Books and Reading*, p. 273.   [2] Walter Pater.
[3] George Saintsbury.

X

INTERPRETATIVE CRITICISM

" Next to invention is the power of interpreting invention : next to beauty the power of appreciating beauty."—ANONY-MOUS.

CONSIDERABLE is heard from time to time about " the higher criticism." What is meant is not always quite clear to readers. It is evident to all that there may be something higher than petty flaw-finding and careless flippancy, ignorant dogmatism and wilful perversion. If not, the art might better become a lost one at an early day. Fortunately there are examples of better performance in the literature of judgment. Such are the common forms which have been noticed already as Impression, Commendation, and Appreciation. Still larger and higher methods are also practised by those who have reached advanced stages in the art, making long strides forward in processes

Use of the term Higher Criticism.

and products. It cannot be said that higher literary criticism is to be found exclusively in books as distinguished from periodicals and journals, since much that has been first printed in serials is found later in more permanent form. The reason why it has taken this form may be on account of the permanent values there are in it, while some appreciations, impressions, and interpretations have passed directly from the author to the book publisher. Whatever their history they will contain certain qualities to which the general sense has attached the epithet " higher."

Primarily, the term belongs to Biblical criticism, being attributed to Eichorn of Gottingen, and applied by him to his rational- *First applied to Biblical criticism.* istic treatment of entire books of the Old Testament, as distinguished from what he called the " lower " criticism of words and passages. This terminology of his was not adopted generally by his own contemporaries, but has been taken up in England and in this country and much talked of during the last ten years with a meaning similar to his own. It is still restricted, for the most part, to the examination of traditional views of Old Testament literature.

Long before Eichorn and as far back as Alexandria in the third century there was a tendency to make divisions of the general art of criticism into " the greater and the less," The Greater that is, judgment about writers in and the Less. poetry and prose, and also about methods of combining letters and syllables in philology. Later there came in other divisions of the general science of criticism, differing with different classifiers almost as much as critics themselves differ. Aside from Art Criticism there have been the Scientific, Philosophical, and Historical, as large and comprehensive classifications. Under the last named Literary Criticism has been reckoned by some, when the questions raised have had reference to genuineness and authenticity of documents. In general, however, while there has prevailed a reflex disposition in some quarters to make the one word Criticism cover all kinds of judgment, the necessity of discrimination has forced itself upon analytic minds, as is seen in the numerous attempts to reach a satisfactory classification. It is as true in the branches as in the main trunk. In Literary Criticism, for example, who can be satisfied to call the judgment displayed in the average book-notice by the same name as that which is shown in an essay of Sainte-Beuve's or Arnold's ? There may be artistic sign-painters, but they do not usually bear the same professional title as Turner and

Millais, nor is the work of both these classes of painters alike called art. It is to be deplored therefore that the epithets Higher and Lower should not be applied to different degrees of the same art of judging rather than to its exercise on objects as far apart as the genuineness of a document, and correctness of a phrase, or the adaptation of diction to the subject in hand. " Great criticism and little," to use an earlier nomenclature, would come nearer the essential character of the two sorts of judgment now in mind; or if a comparison not so invidious would be implied, they might be termed the Greater and the Less.

The main thing is to know what is meant by the distinction. The work of such a critic as Brunetière, contrasted with the laborious prettiness of Beauzée—who, Rivarol remarks, " passed his life between a supine and a gerundive,"—indicates the general notion of the distance between the less and the greater, and of the disparity that may exist under the comprehensive term Criticism. To this should be added the distinction which must necessarily be made between the conventional review article and a critical volume upon Milton or Dante. There are qualities which appear in the more elaborated performance which cannot be incorporated in

Meaning of the Greater and the Less.

the briefer; qualities which the freedom of book-writing inspires and the restrictions of the review-columns prohibit. Chief among these is Interpretation.

By way of definition, the obvious remark may be made here that this word implies three *Interpreta-* things: a literary production, a per-*tion defined.* son who understands it, and other persons who do not understand it so well. The extreme illustrative example is the translation of a document in an unknown tongue into one that is known by the reader, as Cæsar's *Gallic Wars* from Latin into English. But if the book happen to be Aristotle's *Poetic* or Plato's *Republic* there might be, for some readers, need of further interpretation. In like manner sundry English works will bear elucidation, particularly if they deal with specialisms or with common subjects in an abstruse or uncommon way, after the manner of·divers poets and essayists. Such interpretation relates simply to making the writer's meaning clear, so far as he himself has escaped that mistiness of thought which no interpretation can make clear. If he has not escaped it, he cannot expect the critic to make known his dream besides showing the interpretation thereof.

A certain rash impatience in readers might

provoke them to say just here, that an author who cannot think clearly and state his thought with equal lucidity does not deserve interpretation; but much that is of value would have been lost to the world if such counsel had always been followed, beginning with the classics and ending with Browning and Emerson. Interpretation, however, must not be confounded with literal translation as applied to foreign languages or to obscure English. It is not a word-for-word affair in either case. It deals rather with the thought of an author, and this not consecutively, sentence by sentence, nor even paragraph by paragraph, or chapter by chapter. It is a larger process, and therefore justifies its position and rank amidst the " greater criticism."

Its first obligation is to clear up such obscurities as may exist for the ordinary reader; but beyond this clarifying process of the text and letter is the faithful representation of the writer's spirit which lies back of his words and his thoughts as soul lies back of mind, as character underlies deeds, and as life stands behind all bodily activity. This spirit of the author is both the key to interpretation and the first thing to be interpreted, provided his meaning is always obvious. If it is the writer's design to give information for the purpose of increasing knowledge, or of making a vague subject more definite, the controlling influence in the interpretative critic's efforts will be to guide such endeavour in the same direction with a similar purpose. He will try to make what the author says clearer still. He will not make it more obscure by obtruding theories of his own. If he has them, let him make a book of his own. He has no right to mingle them with an interpretation of another man's view to its distortion. How often this is done need not be inquired. The tendency to air one's own sentiments, taking another's for a text, has been well hit off by a writer who says: " I propose to talk of myself in relation to Shakespeare, Racine, Pascal, and Goethe." Fortunately the sentiments of eminent authors are not likely to be greatly harmed by an ordinary critic's interjected views, but lesser writers also have an equal right to fair interpretation.

If they have been successful enough to state their own opinion clearly, they may fairly expect their interpreter to present that opinion to the public as clearly and without alloy. The critic has the right to say what he thinks of the author's opinions and statements of fact, but to substitute his own notions is not interpretation. The man who is telling the people what message an ambassador from a foreign country has been delivering does not substitute his own sentiments about peace or war, unless he wishes to make mischief. Even so attractive a spokesman as John Alden will not speak for himself until Priscilla suggests a change in the object of mediation.

There are doubtless critics whose discourse people listen to with greater interest than to that of any author the critic may chance to take up. When they thus listen it may be safely said that they do so with full knowledge of what they are about. They pick up Arnold or Carlyle, Froude or Taine, not to know what some minor personage has said, of whom these great critics are writing, but to read anything from these writers eminent in the literature of criticism. On the other hand, it may be asserted with equal safety that such masters of their art are sure to be the most faithful of interpreters. They have their own views, but they can afford to be loyal to the authors they are introducing to the public or re-viewing for the public's benefit. It is usually the obscure critic who, like the undistinguished chairman of a lecture-course committee, improves his brief moment on the platform to introduce himself with more or less irrelevant or personal remark about the lecturer. The impersonality which is so much clamoured for by critics might frequently be practised in their interpretations as well as in their signatures.

To be a good interpreter, then, may require considerable self-restraint. The opportunity to eclipse another is tempting, while to assist in one's own eclipse is trying to human infirmity. Here is where the heroism of the profession comes in. Still it is no more than the obvious obligation of the literary interpreter to present another to the best advantage, and keep himself in the background. The grace and skill, the generosity and faithfulness of his presentation will win him his own reward. The reverse of these self-denying virtues may bring him notoriety, but not of the most desirable kind.

Self-restraint in interpreting another.

One of the chief values of interpretation is in making an author's main ideas available by briefer statement. Many readers wish to know the drift of a book only, or to know where its topics may be found at a future day. Persons who never interest themselves to read a treatise on some social or scientific topic are willing to turn aside from their customary lines of thought long enough to read a column or a page, and perhaps will carry away all they need for their present use. To secure such available

Interpreting by condensing in due proportion.

brevity with due proportion requires skill and care in abbreviating; also some conscience lest the author be misrepresented by distortion.   It is as easy to magnify the insignificant and to dwarf the important as to paste two photographs together and make a comic caricature with a giant's head on a brownie's body, or the reverse.   Only one meaner thing can be done by a critic, and that is to make some slip of the pen the subject of the major part of a critique,—an enlarged finger to stand for the entire body of the man.   No acumen is required to discover lameness in a passer-by, and but little good breeding not to gaze at him until the attention of the whole street is directed to his infirmity, and to that alone.

Leaving such critical manners to boors, it may be said that proportionate condensation shows both the skill and the conscience of a reviewer.   First, his **Abridgment.** skill; of which abridgment requires more than enlargement, and leaves little room for personal additions.   Many an artist can copy a square mile of landscape upon a square foot of canvas: not everyone can keep the proportion of foreground and background, of tree and mountain, leaving out the unimportant bush and putting in the important copse, and giving all principal objects the relative space they oc-

cupy on the retina or on the camera plate.
This may be too much to ask of the reviewer,
but not if he professes to be an artist in his
work. And in a day when artist tailors and
artist caterers and tonsorial artists are advertised, is it too much to expect that there should
be artist critics ?—and if artists, they should
practise the first principles of practical art,
namely, reduction in proportion. Even an
artist photographer does that, and the eye
does it before the photographer or the artist
proper. It may not be unfair to ask as much
from the critic, making due allowance for the
greater difficulty of his task, and the tempta-
tions to distort, more numerous than those
which beset the painter of landscapes. It is
not to be denied that the critic, like the skilful
artist, may make an ideal production out of
one that is not, by omitting, supplying, and
replacing; but he is seldom called upon to improve upon his author by this process. All the
author can ask is to be interpreted in miniature
and in due proportion. If his faults drop out
in the process, well and good; but he may
insist that they be not magnified.

The conscientious critic accordingly studies
proportionate reduction, and to give each important division of the book in hand the relative attention which its importance demands.

If his space be limited, as it usually is, he will pay greater consideration to the large divisions and main thoughts and general pro-positions than to minor remarks and statements, if he is a just interpre-ter.   If he is not, he will pitch upon some obscure inaccuracy, some aside reflection, some wayside and momentary departure from the main thoroughfare of the author's thought and give it a prominence which is both undue and unfair.

Every reader of book-notices will recall examples of such exposition in which he might have inferred that the entire volume was an elaboration of some inaccuracy, or that the author had expended his time and strength upon the defence of a misapprehension.   Meantime his real purpose and the burden of his message to the reading world is forgotten, or passed over with mere mention in the critic's greater achievement of discovering a mistake of little consequence.   In this way the fly in the amber becomes of greater importance than the amber itself, and a work is of value to the reviewer in proportion to the number of flaws he can find in it.

If such practice of interpretation should largely prevail, current literature would present a sorry aspect to the inquirer after something worth reading. A moderate fault-finder would not need to search far nor wait long to detect slips of the memory and of the pen in writers who are doing good service in the field of letters. Volumes have been compiled by the hypercritical to prove that all Homers nod, and that prosy Platos may be caught napping. One of these Argus-eyed inspectors reports lapses in the use of the verb by Sydney Smith, Sir Samuel Romily, Ruskin, *The Spectator*, Coleridge, Landor, Leslie Stephen, Buckle, Bulwer, not to mention other eminent writers in Great Britain and America. As it is not the habit of such writers to misplace their auxiliary verbs, or to indulge in careless and false apposition, a critic would be misinterpreting their purpose and underrating their value to magnify such inaccuracies. Besides he might be depriving the world of much good literature if his representations should happen to have any great value to readers. Even so gross an error as the occasional lack of concord between subject and verb has not greatly impaired the usefulness and reputation of Charles Kingsley, De Quincey, Matthew Arnold, Robert Buchanan, F. W. Newman, J. S. Mill, Miss Mitford, G. H. Lewes, Lord Houghton, B. D'Israeli, besides distinguished writers in British reviews, and

Effect of distortion upon literature at large.

American writers in the past and present whose names are withheld for obvious reasons.[1] No flaw-hunter need go far afield to obtain a large and respectable collection, enough to condemn most of the literature of our time if little faults be placed under his microscope and excellences be examined with the glass reversed. It is a more difficult task to interpret such literature by the high purpose and large execution that its makers have given to it than to discover an incorrect reference of a relative pronoun, the misuse of a conjunction, or even the misstatement of an unimportant fact. Sometimes the spirit of an author is too fine or his motive too lofty to be apprehended by the finical into whose hands his writings happen to fall for interpretation. In that case the least that can be done is to accord in general terms the elevation of spirit and motive which may be recognised, if not appreciated and analysed. It is not needful to measure the exact altitude of an Alp to be impressed with its sublimity. On the other hand, it is not necessary to deny its majesty and to assume indifference to its awe-inspiring features.

Just interpretation, then, must begin with sympathetic understanding and be carried on

[1] See Hodgson's *Errors in the Use of English* and similar handbooks.

11

with fair and proportionate representation. To this must be added a definite knowledge of

A writer's constituency to be considered. the constituency for whom such interpretation is to be made. Among them there will be a diversity of capacity and ability which must be taken into account. A greater number than the critic may suppose will be able to read without an interpreter at all when they get at the author by themselves; but the critic is now regarded as a scout to report what are the new arrivals in the field of letters, and to say what they are like. Other readers will so differ in the readiness of their apprehension that what can be made plain to another by a few suggestive words must be explained at length to them. In short, the difficulties of interpretation may be many more on the side of the reading public than on that of the author. There are prejudices which must not be disturbed, oppositions which must not be roused, natural antagonisms which must be allayed before an author can get justice at the hands of the multitude. For this multitude never surrenders its democratic privilege of serving on a jury, and of having its own inherited prejudices, even if it can take oath that it has never expressed an opinion in the case or read the newspaper's opinion. No one is better able to deal with the popular understanding than the journalists who have an opportunity to test its resources with each issue of their sheet. Letters to the editor and the talk of the street, the market, and the fireside are the best of indicators, as the subscription list is the most practical. Hence it is, perhaps, that the most successful interpreters of literature to the people have come up through the reflex education of this same constituency, concurrent and recalcitrant by turns. This does not imply that the critic is to follow popular taste and senti- Its judgment ment, while pretending to lead it, as and demand. is sometimes the case in politics and other matters. He need have no obligation to represent an author otherwise than he has represented himself. The rest he may confidently trust to an intelligent public who will not thank him for misinterpretation. What they will be grateful for is, such a general notion of what the author has written that they may determine whether they wish to read all that he has said, or to pursue the subject no further under his guidance. Of course this is a position of power and responsibility on the part of the person who stands between authors and readers. Power to direct or to mislead, for gain or for loss, for knowledge or for ignorance. The responsibility also is twofold: to the reader that he be rightly informed; to the author that he be justly represented. How far such a sense of responsiblity prevails among the introducers of books to the public is a matter of conjecture merely. As in other matters the degree of it varies with different persons, and with the same persons at different times. There are some who are conscientious in the discharge of their trust, and others whose personal interests and prejudices, likes and dislikes, purposes and ambitions give a bias and twist to their judgment, and therefore misrepresentation to the author they are interpreting. After all, it is possible that no one so well as the author himself can explain what may not be at first understood. Certainly no one should be better able to give a proportionate abstract, compend, or precis of what he has written at length. It is better, however, that some one else should do this, in order that the writer may see how he has been understood by others, and how far he has succeeded in representing the thought which was presented to him. If it requires too much explanation and interpretation he has partially failed. If it has been honestly misapprehended, the failure is greater still. The remedy and the prevention are in making himself so clear that none but a perversely in-

clined interpreter can find more than one meaning in his words, and have no difficulty in
communicating that meaning to the public.
Nevertheless he will get wholesome suggestion
and possibly comfort if he keep always in mind
the boast of Richelieu: '' Show me six lines
written by the most honest man in the world
and I will find enough therein to hang him.''
Perspicuity in the author, honesty in the interpreter, and belief on the part of the reader, are
three factors which readily combine to serve
the interests of literature with rapidity and
effectiveness. The writer soon comes to understand what the public demands in his line, and
readers find who will best meet their demand;
and this knowledge on both sides is greatly
hastened by the intermediate agency of the
judicious and faithful interpretative critic.

XI

COMPARATIVE CRITICISM

The effort of criticism in our time has been to see things as they are, without partiality and without obtrusion of personal liking or disliking.—DOWDEN.

IN a sense all criticism is comparative, as all judgment is an act of the comparative faculty. A product of human endeavour is good or bad, better or worse, relatively to some fixed or movable standard. In the domain of higher criticism, however, there is an order of it which may be called comparative in the sense that anatomy or philology is so named when the one deals with the differences in classes, orders, and species of the animal kingdom, in their structure and organisation, and the other with the growth, composition, and decay of different languages. In a similar manner criticism has, in its comparative phase, the classification of a world of literature into classes, orders, and

Significance of the term as here employed.

species, and the subsequent assigning to each individual author his proper place according to the predominant characteristics of his work. This procedure is in harmony with the method of all comparative science, which, according to its definition, " undertakes to deduce comprehensive scientific results from a comparison of various groups of related phenomena."

The beginnings of this process are simple. The ordinary reader picks up a book, and in a moment says, this is history or fiction, biography or science, philosophy or theology. *Inductive process first.* He turns to the title-page to find the author's name, and, whatever may be his occupation or other literary work, the author is for the time and in the instance of this present book an historian or biographer, novelist or philosopher. Remarkable intelligence is not requisite for such classification, and the most ordinary acquaintance with literary history suffices to place Aristotle and Plato among the philosophers, Gibbon and Hume among the historians, Scott and Dickens among the novelists. As the circle widens in each of these departments, or as the list of authors lengthens, it becomes more and more difficult to say where to place such names as are obscure through distance or mediocrity. Cleanthes, Pelezius, Felix Plater, Rhasis, Mesue, Syracides, and

all the undistinguished company with whom
Robert Burton is so familiar in his comparative
Anatomy of Melancholy, are not classified in
these days without the assistance of a biographical dictionary, nor always with it; and
there are some modern writers whose names
are more familiar in the general domain of
literature than the particular departments of it
to which they belong.

A primary step in comparative criticism is
analysis. That there may be no misunderstanding of the meaning of the word
Analysis. as here used, let this illustration of
it be employed. Among the varied objects in
a landscape I behold something with leaves,
branches, and trunk united as a whole. I form
the notion of a tree, or, having the notion already formed, I compare this object with that
notion, unconsciously, perhaps, and know that
it is a tree, and not a rock or a river or a house.
Its place is assigned with all others of its class
and not in any other class. This is its first
and largest classification. Subsequently there
will be further analysis and other classification,
as an oak, maple, or elm tree, with the numerous varieties of each, in which the process in-
creases in difficulty and out of all proportion to
the simplicity of its beginning. The same
procedure obtains in the world of books, after

books have been separated from all other things in the material world. A volume is opened which treats of what was done years or centuries ago.   By this token it corresponds to the accepted notion of history, and its author is for the time an historian, and his place in literature among the historians of all time.   He is in a large room in which further discrimination will find for him a definite position according to his nationality, or subject, or treatment of it, or any or many other qualifications and conditions.   But the first process will be analytic and discriminative.

In later analysis the difficulties of comparative criticism begin, as has already been intimated with respect to obscure authors.   There are in the intellectual character of every author idiosyncrasies which separate him from others of his class more or less remotely.   His literary product will differ by one or several shades from the writers with whom he is commonly ranked.   The degree of this variation will be determined by the fidelity of his work to his own standards and convictions.   If this diversity be strongly marked it may constitute good and sufficient reason to place him in a subdivision of his own, like Thoreau in his hut at Walden Pond, Percival in his windowless house, or where his fellow-workers will be few and unlike him, as in the instance of Walt Whitman in Camden. "Seats of the mighty" are always reserved for genius; but men of talent and ordinary ability sometimes display an individuality which entitles them to the distinction that belongs to species, or at least to a variety. For example, Shakespeare, being of the class poetic, order dramatic, and tribe Elizabethan, may have a genius so preëminent as to isolate him from all his tribe, far enough at least to place him at the head of the table at the Mermaid Tavern. This, however, does not of necessity make one common and undistinguished herd of Marlowe, Jonson, Chapman, Peele, Greene, Decker, Webster, Marston, Middleton, Beaumont, Fletcher, and the rest of the wits in that illustrious company. They may not have been differentiated far enough from one another to constitute distinct species, still less separate orders, but here and there one established sufficient variation from type to demand a niche by himself beyond our last analysis. The critic, for instance, who finds nothing so fine in English poetry as Marlowe's lines—

> " Is this the face that launched a thousand ships,
> And fired the topless towers of Ilium ?"

will have a special recess reserved in the Poet's

Corner in the Abbey where he would not place Ford and Lodge.   In like manner another critic [1] of our time would assign to Jonson a nook of his own for " founding a school of treatment of which the law is caricature."   In this manner analysis may proceed until it does not serve the purposes of comparison so much as of distinction and separation, which is in a sense the other and reverse side of comparison, showing the unlikeness instead of the likeness of authors and their works.

This process is both good and necessary, to whatever it may lead.   A general classification of writers and books helps to direct criticism into proper channels and to limit it within definite bounds.   If the work to be estimated is a history, *Classification preparatory to judicial criticism.* it will not be mistaken for fiction and judged by the laws of romance writing.   If a scientific treatise, a poetic treatment of its subject will not be expected.   If a biographical essay, the methods of character drawing appropriate to a novel will not be demanded.   Labour is thus both saved and properly adjusted to the business in hand, vagaries avoided, and irrelevancies made inexcusable.

The one danger in pursuing the analytic

---

[1] R. G. Moulton *Shakespeare as a Dramatic Artist*, Introduction.

method too far is that judicial comparison may

Dangers of the analytic method. be entirely lost sight of. When idiosyncrasies are discovered and magnified into originality, and eccentricity is mistaken for genius, making an author a law unto himself because he has broken with the traditions of his tribe, the next step is to say that he must not be compared with his fellows, nor be judged by the law of his province. Criticism then becomes classification and nothing more. It has no more to do with relative merit than the lumber sorter has to do with the relative value of pine, oak, and mahogany. He puts each board with its own kind, for its own uses. He cannot say that one is better than another. Mahogany may bring a higher price than spruce, but it is not so valuable for flooring and sheathing; and the dealer in it may have less profits than the dealer in hemlock. Accordingly the analysis of a lumber-yard ends in classification, a pile of pine here, of chestnut there, of oak or of maple elsewhere. Comparison has no place at first in this assorting process. Criticism ends with induction, and judgment with distinguishing between one class and another according to this method.

After this is done the comparison between good and poor individuals in the same class begins, and a further separation into first-, second-, and third-rate quality takes place. The criticism which was discriminative with respect to kinds, now becomes comparative in regard to degree of excellence. Is this piece of lumber as sound as another, or as the best that grows ? Is the grain as straight and the texture as firm, the marking as fine ? Will it meet the builder's wants and satisfy his artistic sense ?

The parallel has been carried far enough to make clear the limits of comparative criticism in literature, if it be confined to inductive classification. Its usefulness has been shown in simplifying and directing the labours of the critic by confining his attention and expectations to one class of work at a time. If it end with this, there can be but little literary acumen required. Only an ordinary reader's knowledge is needed to assort books according to their subject-matter, corresponding to the countryman's knowledge of woodcraft. This may be judgment, but it is of a primitive kind. More is requisite to discover and discriminate variations from the ordinary type, as when " by a cross-fertilisation of two existing species a third, including the features of both, is added to literature." Still no degree of excellence higher or lower is implied in such discrimination and assignment. The hybrid fruit of a sweet scion grafted into a sour apple-tree must not be compared for excellence with either of the original stocks, according to the rule of classification. It is a new variety standing on its own merits. I may like it or not like it and say so; but I must not say I like it less than some other or better than another still.

The best, then, that can be said for this sort of classifying criticism is, that it prepares the way admirably for judicial criticism—the comparison of individuals with one another, or with absolute standards after they have been reduced to the lowest terms of classification. When historians, for example, have been divided and set off by national and time characteristics until those who have written histories of the United States are grouped together, and from them those who have written histories of our Constitution are assembled by themselves, then an important preliminary work has been accomplished. This is a work requiring judgment based upon knowledge acquired by reading and study, especially if some one of them has earned a distinct place for himself by a unique and effective method of treatment. To discover this and make it apparent to others will require discrimination and clear presentation. Dividing the members of a small group of writers on the constitutional history of our nation, there are differences of profundity in views, of literary sense and faculty, of diction, movement, and proportion that are subjects of a judgment not like that which merely classifies. Curtis and Von Holst are easily assigned their place among writers of constitutional history; but a comparison of their respective literary qualities is not so readily made. It is not a matter of kind so much as of degrees of excellence in the same kind of composition; not whether both Prescott and Motley are transcribers of facts relating to Spanish dominion, and are therefore to be put into the same category as historians, and nothing more to be said about them, as whether, for example, their facts gain or lose in communication by the respective style of each author.

Must it not be conceded, therefore, that inductive comparison and classification of authors, while preliminary to a further com- _Judicial more_ parison of members of the same _difficult._ group, cannot be ranked with the judicial method in the diversity and intricacy of its processes, and in the variety of qualities, intellectual and æsthetic, which it has to take into consideration ? Some judgment is required to classify, but much more to characterise the individual author who has been relegated to his genus and species. What is commonly understood as criticism begins here. It is not enough for the critic to say, This author is a poet of the first or fourth class who has written on such and such themes. Almost any reader can compete with that sort of criticism. He wants someone to tell him what is true about the poet, but not obvious at first sight to every reader: that his verse, for example, derives its pleasure-giving power from the highest and most unfailing sources; that his imagination is at home in ethereal regions; his diction unalterable without injury to the finer sense; his spirit so full of human sympathy that readers are called back again and again to its expression in measures that never tire, abiding in the memory as household words, or as scriptural phrases that are marred by mending. By such interpretation the critic passes on from comparative to appreciative judgment, or even condemnatory, if there be a falling short of the best. The insight and the effort required are much greater where such interpretation is to be made, or the endowments of one writer are to be compared with those of another in these respects. But first in order of time is the allotment of each writer to his own company, and often of the same author to different companies according to the work he is producing, be it verse or prose, history or philosophy, biography or fiction. Then judicial criticism will follow as a natural sequence, carrying the same principle of comparison from the class to the individual.

It would seem that in this legitimate transfer and succession might be found a solution of the vexed controversy between advocates of the inductive and judicial methods respectively. Primordially these both rest upon the Comparative Faculty, the basis of our knowledge of things similar or unlike. Eliminate either process from criticism, and the result is partial and one-sided. Retain both, and literature is classified according to its kinds, and the work in each kind according to its quality.

Controversy between the two methods.

There is a still broader sense in which comparison is applied to criticism. It is when the objects of it are not so much different kinds of literature to be compared in order to classification, as the same kinds in different times, nations, or circumstances in order to discover how near any given example approaches what is best in all examples. In this procedure the standard which is established is an exalted one. It is a result of the combined efforts of the race in

Broader meaning of the term.

12

many centuries and many lands. The nearest parallel is found in the work of the sculptor who travels far and inquires much to find a noble head, a fair face, a shapely hand, and brings home his copies of all when found to incorporate into his ideal statue. To this in turn he may refer the aspirant to excellence in any feature; for very few will be ambitious enough to set up Belviderian claims.

In like manner the comparative method, in this large phase of it, sends the critic into many lands and literatures to see in what garb one writer and another have clothed common sentiments of the human race or its uncommon experiences. The method of Homer and Virgil, of Æschylus and Shakespeare, of Milton and Dante, will first be ascertained and then compared to note which has surpassed another or all the others, and which accordingly shall furnish, until he himself shall be outdone, the best that has been thought and written in a given direction. It may not be the best form or the most advanced thought for the present time, as the ships and the arms and the speeches of the *Iliad* would not answer for the navies, the armies, and the assemblies of the present day. But the Answer of Achilles to the Embassy, the description of his shield, the account of the

Parting of Hector and Andromache, all help one to estimate similar passages in later classics from Virgil to Tennyson.   One may prefer this poet or passage to that, but there is something which is common as well as much that is individual in the greater suns which flash their signals to each other across the spaces and times, past planets reflecting their light, past the meteors of a moment, and all eccentric and evanescent wanderers in the heavens. They are central sources of life and movement in their respective systems, and for this reason comparable with one another and interpretative each of the others' works and ways.

To such comparative criticism the first essential is some knowledge of the authors who represent the principal periods which *Wide reading* contribute to the general stock of *necessary.* the best literary attainment. To obtain this knowledge one must read widely. The ability to do this and do it well is almost as much of a gift as the critical faculty itself.   It is not the omnivorous reader that is here meant, who devours all things both great and small, coarse and fine, who reads anything that comes in his way for the sake of reading. He may get an incidental advantage out of knowing that there is poor stuff in abundance and easy of access ; but the habits of the ostrich are not known to have made that bird a comparative critic in foods. Neither is it the dainty humming-bird skimmer over the fields of literature, picking and tasting here and there, perhaps not even the laborious bee, freighted with elegant extracts and apothegms, quotations and statistics. It is rather the reader who has the knack of reading by the page instead of by the line, grasping the thoughts of an author by the handful, rejecting the worthless and retaining the valuable with the instinctive precision of an expert in coins. Such a reader, while he must move rapidly over large areas of literature if he is to make his comparisons comprehensive, will also need to know his ground well enough to discern similarities and differences however far apart they may exist. He will see where Homer and Milton resemble each other, when Sophocles and Shakespeare touch a common chord.

The wider, too, such reading is, the more trustworthy will be the results of comparison. The classics of all ages will furnish occupation for an ordinary reader for years, but there is much that is not classic that will be of service to the comparative student of literature. Possibly the work of talent as distinguished from

that of genius affords the best material for a
just estimate of any literary age. Certainly it
is always abundant while the other is rare and
infrequent. By which, for instance, shall the
last quarter of this century be judged ? Is
there a single light-giver of even the third
magnitude above the horizon as the century
closes, beginning with poetry and ending with
criticism ? Owing to creditable performance
in what may be called original or creative
work earlier in the century, it is natural to
look for special activity and excellence along
critical lines, according to the customary sequence. If any exception is to be taken to
what is implied in the above questions it may
be in the instance of the greater criticism
which is appearing from time to time abroad
and here and there in this country.

Still for a true estimate of the literature of
the present decade the elements to be chiefly
considered are talent and mediocrity rather
than genius. Therefore their products will
have to be read by the critic who is taking a
comparative view of nineteenth-century literature. There is no lack of material. He may
find the riches of its abundance very embarrassing as he reads on and on. Amidst so much
it will be difficult to get that perspective view
which is essential to the truest comparison.

This, indeed, is always the critic's most perplexing problem. The past is determined and settled. Its rubbish is disposed of. Its greater values have found their place and have been assigned their rank. But in the literature that is now making it is as difficult to discover permanent values as to recognise the heroic in the every-day life around us. Comparative criticism in the twentieth century will do this easier and better. " You must stand far off to judge St. Peter's." It may be needful to stand off as far to determine values that lurk beneath less pretentious structures.

Such comparative criticism if done wisely and well has its own peculiar worth. Its standards are broad and ought to be high. Looking beyond the local

Value of higher comparison.

and temporary and transient in every phase and fashion of literature, it finds the. perpetual elements in each and discards the ephemeral and accidental. With these go much that invites carping criticism, furnishing opportunity for mere fault-finding. Larger methods of comparison treat such features only as curious coincidences, while the cardinal virtues are recognised as tokens of unity and kinship of intellectual orders of nobility the world over and in all time. The wider its researches the more satisfactory its conclusions become, and

the stronger its hope that the best standards
will ultimately prevail, since they have invari-
ably outlasted the transitory and the inferior.
The broad-arrow mark upon them all is the
simplicity and grandeur of nature, as distinguished from artificiality and passing conceits.
These attract attention in their day and country.   The others appeal to humanity at large,
the best of it, in all countries and in all times.

XII

HISTORICAL CRITICISM

" It is a fallacy to treat as a blemish of the man what is the tincture of the age."—LOWELL.

THE older criticism previous to Villemain was largely a matter of comparison with classic standards, with an occasional revolt to personal preferences and such individual au- thority as eminence in letters might confer. The author was regarded most often as a sample of a common humanity which changes but little in the lapse of ages and varies in essentials still less in different countries. Because men ate, drank, and slept, married, builded, and fought the world over, it was accepted with too little considera-tion that under similar conditions the same re-sults would always follow. The next step in this reasoning was to say that, if they did not follow, something must be wrong and abnormal, and therefore subject to judgment and criticism,

184

As applied to literature, this method would demand, if consistent with itself, that such history as Herodotus or Thucydides wrote in Greece in the fifth century B.C. should be written by Tacitus at Rome five hundred years later, and by Froissart in France fourteen centuries later still; for is not human nature an unchanging element, and the surface of the globe.and the order of the seasons and the pursuits of mankind other constant quantities in the problem of production ? The human mind beyond all variations of times and places must be the same in its faculties however much the development and power of these may vary in different persons. The productions of the best in all centuries and countries should therefore be rated by similar rules, and writers be judged by the laws of mind which are assumed to be unchanging. So reasoned the elders.

It is singular that certain wide differences in the expression of traits that are common did not convey their instruction to early critics. It is true that human nature the world over runs to building, but how diverse are the styles of architecture, themselves shaped by differences of climate. Hunger is a common experience of all races, but some would go hungry to the starvation point before they would eat the others' delicacies. The weapons with which the common instinct of fighting is exercised or the higher instinct of patriotism expressed range from the club to the machine gun. While, then, there are common impulses of a common human nature, the most elementary and universal of them have the greatest variety of manifestation. In estimating these no one thinks of setting up a standard of judgment apart from such allowances as are made for diversity of civilisation and enlightenment, of advantages and history. Classification is made almost unconsciously, but judgment is not so much between classes as individuals in each class. The hut and the arrows of one Bushman are compared justly with those of another, but not with the villa and the rifle of an Englishman or American.

Criticism was unaccountably slow in recognising this principle in literature which common sense dictated in everything else, namely, that some account must be taken of environment in judging of the productions of any age, nation, or person. It is the law of allowances as distinguished from absolute law; such allowance as men are always making for the moderate performances of those who have had little education and training, and every circum-

Late recognition of this principle by critics.

stance against them, and on the other hand the great demands they make of those whom everything favours and of whom they have a right to expect much. Thus it becomes like that flexible and adaptive element in the administration of a justice which itself is supposed to be inflexible and unalterable, with one penalty for all offenders according to the offence. Instead, in the actual application by a just judge, it is not unaffected by his knowledge and consideration of mitigating circumstances, or again of great light which has been sinned against.

When this principle comes to be applied to literature in its historical development there is much to be taken into account. It would be unfair to expect the same qualities, and in a similar degree, *Allowances for diversity of advantages.* from the early bards of a nation as from its later poets, or from the bardic poetry of the race as from the epic and dramatic development of its maturer ages. For in all the centuries there has been time for growth and the advantages of experiment and examples to follow and improve upon. Each generation has the shoulders of all its predecessors for its ladder, and while it should not despise the steps by which it has climbed to eminence, the responsibility of attaining the highest possible cannot be avoided. Comparison, then, may not be invidious, although it must be unavoidable. But if comparison is made, allowances are also to be made by that method which brings history to the help of criticism.

There will always be more or less of discussion as to how far genius is affected by its surroundings, and mind by material things. Great abilities are doubtless bound to find expression under favourable and unfavourable conditions alike. The great English epic poet will forget his poverty and blindness for hours in his vision of Paradise, and Seneca will divert himself by writing the praises of poverty on a table of gold. Still literature is not entirely a product of mere personality apart from surroundings.

Genius as affected by its surroundings.

Beginning with thought, it is apparent that the meditations of one age are not altogether like those of another. Primitive writers dwelt much upon phases of nature, particularly its melancholy moods, upon war and its heroes, upon wanderings and discovery, upon events and occurrences little and great together. Later, causes and consequences began to be traced and human nature to be observed, until at length literature became introspective and philosophic. Lay Hesiod and Wordsworth side by side, or Herodotus and Macaulay, Sophocles and Ben

In thought.

Jonson, and the thoughts of the last poet, historian, and dramatist will not be as those of the first, although running similarly upon nature, human nature, and history.

Still more evident is this diversity in the expression of thought, termed Style; as great almost as in the particular of language, and after making due allowance for difference in tongue and dialect. Is it possible to account for such variation on the hypothesis of idiosyncrasy and personality and individuality in one writer and another ? If so, why in the repetitions of history should not Euripides reappear in any century, or Thucydides or Plato ? Instead, it is found that the variations are greater between centuries remote from one another than between men of talent in the same century. Æschylus, Euripides, and Sophocles do not differ from each other, nor Shakespeare, Marlowe, and Ben Jonson, so much as the one group differs from the other group in both habits of thinking and modes of expression. What gives more distinction to a generation or school of writers than to the individual members of it, if it be not characteristics which belong to one century or country and not to the other ? Could the *Iliad* have been written in the Restoration Period, or could Homer have composed the *Dunciad?* Could the *Pilgrim's Progress* have been imagined before the beginning of the Christian era, or much of hymnody before the establishment of mediæval ecclesiasticism ? Certainly between the ancient and modern world there is a broad distinction in thinking which finds a corresponding divergence in expression.

These differences would not need emphasising if there were not indications of a reaction from the fundamental idea of historical criticism; men are returning to personality as a sufficient reason for variations in the literary product of different ages over and above language diversity. To be sure it is a comparatively recent explanation of variety; but criticism is a progressive science, or art if one prefers to call it so, and the new explanation ought to be better than the old, as the Copernican theory is better than the Ptolemaic. The old criticism looked at literature as the product of Mind separated from nation, century, almost from body. Intellect was in this way compared with intellect as star might be with star on the primitive supposition that they were golden nails studding the vault above. Their size was rated by their appearance, and no factor of distance or source of light was taken into account. This childish standard is convenient but unfavourable to distant suns and flattering to our own sun and to the family of reflectors paying it their homage.

The new criticism is vastly more difficult and becomes increasingly complicated the farther it pursues its labours.   History has to be studied as well as literature, and literature itself in the light of history.   Each becomes explanatory of the other and full of cross-references and corroborations.   Light from unexpected coincidences is shed upon the event in one case, and upon the text of poem or narration in the other.   The history of literature itself thus serves the history of an age, and the story of this in turn renders a reciprocal service to letters.   For example, the annals of Herodotus and Thucydides throw light upon the dramatic literature of the Periclean age, and this again is a large commentary upon the intellectual movements consequent upon the Persian wars. The Elizabethan dramatists cannot be adequately estimated without a study of the causes which made their age one of enlargement and grandeur, whether in the direction of the revival of learning and Italian studies, or in that of maritime conquest and remote discovery. If Strachey's note of a hurricane off the Bermudas found its way into Shakespeare's *Tem-*

pest, it may serve to illustrate the rousing of men's minds in those stirring times which found their fittest expression in dramatic forms. The age itself was full of comedy, history, and tragedy, and its best historians are the group which crystallised its spirit into dramatic literature. At the time these dramas educated the poulace; now they are the record of that active century. Its deeds and its books explain each other.

In a measure this is true of any book in any time. The age in which it was written will account for any departures from whatever belongs to universal types of mind and expression. " I love," " I hate," " I am hungry," may express common feelings and be common words in all lands among all men, with a few other common experiences and sentiments. Beyond these begin the variations which different climes, ages, and cultures make, to be understood only by the knowledge of such diverse influences. Why the *Iliad* was not *Paradise Lost*, and the *Æneid* the *Divine Comedy*, and the *Agamemnon Hamlet;* why, in a word, genius should not always produce uniformly, when it is so uniform in its essential features, is best explained by that criticism which takes account of history. Personal variations are not sufficient, and a writer is always enough the child of his time to be controlled in some measure by the forces and the fashions of his time. He may be in the forefront of it, but not in the next century, nor in the last, except in so far as genius is timeless. He may help to control the literary customs and character of the next age, especially its language, and prolong the ideas which have ruled him, but he is none the less the creature of these dominating forces. The Elizabethan dramatists did much to perpetuate the language they employed, but they were nevertheless the offspring of their time, and were inspired by its spirit.

These forces are what historical criticism endeavours to ascertain in any product it considers worth the investigation. How much of this production is due to Mind in the abstract, and how much do its peculiar features owe to the formative influences that have operated upon genius or talent? *The problem of historical criticism.*

In answering this question it is not necessary to give the preponderance to racial, momentary, or environing influences, as Taine is inclined to, but on the other hand these cannot be overlooked. The man and writer of to-day cannot resist the moulding forces of the present time, its literary habits, its moral atmosphere, its *Environment cannot be disregarded.*

special ambitions, its trend of thought. The same is true of every author of eminence in his time. To know the characteristics of that time is to understand one half the work and mind of genius and the whole of the ordinary man's mind and work. This is only another way of transposing one's self to the author's point of vision—the first requisite of the best criticism. The critic moves into the author's town, sees his neighbours, listens to their talk, weighs the motives that rule them in peace and in war, in their dealings with their fellow-citizens and foreigners. He begins to understand why the man is what he is and why he writes as he does. Perhaps he gets a glimpse of his bookshelves. If so, he will guess what portions of the past have entered into competition with present forces in the books that have influenced thought or style. All these agencies together working upon original Mind —itself often a thing of inheritance—give a considerable sameness to the writers of any particular age.

More of their diversities also may be due to differences of surrounding than is always conceded. Competence or poverty, good fortune or adversity, manifold or meagre advantages, are things to which genius is not insensible, and which make or mar the success of the ordinary man of letters. Can the sunshine in the writings of Irving be entirely accounted for by the sweetness of his disposition, or the shadow in Poe's by a gloomy spirit ? Did the Berkshire Hills lend a November chill to Bryant's verse, or the meadows of the Charles, the amenities of Cambridge, and the towns of southern Europe make Longfellow's poems full of lore and loving-kindness ? Subtler influences of inheritance and environment might be added which historical criticism will not pass over in its philosophic mood of accounting for the final product. But in all its computations there will be considered as a main element, that power which in its last extremity lives and labours independent of its surroundings and absorbed in its own activity. Environment may colour the creative faculty as climate dyes the skin, but beneath his complexion and amidst his surroundings man lives, loves, and toils, and Mind creates and re-creates with equal freedom in Bedford jail or in Ayrshire fields. Nevertheless, the great Allegory is better understood as one stands on the Ouse bridge, and the peasant's song from the Brig o' Doon. Suppose that either were summoned to judgment at some Greek, French, or German Areopagus to be tried by an absolute classicism or romanticism with no prison or plough in the background. Or again, let these authors change places and fortunes, and imagine the variations in the story and the song.

In a similar manner the historical method will have its allowances to make when it traces literatures from their beginnings to their highest development. There may be an unlooked-for manifestation of genius at the outset, but no one will expect the same performance amidst rude conditions of barbarism as when it is surrounded by the refinements of a later civilisation. Cædmon and Milton may have each had the same general basic thought of the Fall of Man in mind, but something more than natural gifts must be considered when the vast difference is noted in the treatment of this topic by the two poets. It is this phase of historical criticism which strengthens the theory that genius is, in its ultimate development, partly the product of cultivation. If, on the opposite hypothesis, it is a possible accident of any age, why is it not found in full flower in primitive and uncultivated centuries ? Or again, if due allowances are made, shall it be said, for example, that the author of Beowulf's heroic poem must be rated in the same class with the author of the great English epic ? One alternative or the other will be accepted

The historical method as applied to development of literatures.

by those who pass judgment upon the literary products of different centuries with their respective characteristics in mind. But facts seem to favour cultivation as essential to what is commonly called genius.

As usual the truth lies midway between extremes. Environment does not make men nor their minds; but it may change their complexion, make them weak or strong, gentle or harsh, contented or aggressive. It may augment ordinary abilities, or enervate genius itself. Therefore it is the business of criticism to become historical in its habits of investigation in proportion as it expects to be considered both exact and just. It will find the man and also his dwelling-place in space and time, the men with whom he talked, the laws under which he lived, the religion that prevailed, the ideas which were dominant. These will be as marginal notes explaining what of himself the author chooses to reveal. They may illumine his reserves and fill out his intimations. All this helps exactness. It also contributes to justice. For every man has a right to be judged by the laws of his country and with the men of his generation and according to his light. At least this is what men hope is ideal judgment. Accordingly they do not condemn the fourteenth-century Chaucer for what would be glaring faults in the nineteenth century, nor do they excuse a modern poet when he imitates decadences two thousand years old.

As has been remarked, the approach to this historical method was late and slow. From Germany to France and from both countries to England the idea moved with the fortunes attending every new system, encountering opposition from conservative custom, and meeting with favour from hospitable liberality. Goethe at Weimar, Villemain in Paris, and Jeffrey in Edinburgh were its pioneer expositors, although predecessors, like Dryden, descried its coming. To Carlyle, however, belongs the credit of developing and illustrating this method among English-speaking people. He had a long and hard fight of it, but everybody knows his eminent qualifications for battle and how well he cultivated his gifts in this direction. It was an instance where championship of the foreigner did good service to the native land and for the criticism which needed an infusion of fresh ideas. By such service he became himself the foremost British critic of his time; not merely because he was a born judge of character and literature, but also because he lived and worked in a rarer critical atmosphere than he found even on his

Growth of historical criticism.

Scottish hills. Protesting against what was insular, and going beyond the limits of the present or any single age in all literature, he took large views of men and books and the influences which made them; that is, when those books and men and even nations, as in the case of our own, did not run counter to the prejudices of Thomas Carlyle. But this was his weak side. When he rose above himself and his politics his outlook was wide and far, and many things entered into his estimate of an author besides the printed page.

What this large view of literature did for Carlyle a similar disposition may do for any critical student of books and writers. It will give him clearer and juster impressions, fairer and more charitable understanding, deeper knowledge and profounder sympathy, whatever these may be worth to him and to the author. Incidentally he will find his stores of historical and literary information vastly increased, if he follow the leadings which this method maps out. Not, of course, without the labour which it implies, and involves; but what good thing is gained without labour? If, however, there is a desire to know the spirit of an age, so often concealed under a body of facts, events, or commonplace life, nothing will so reveal it as

its writings, nor anything explain them in turn
like contemporary activities.　An adequate
knowledge of the Revolution and the Restoration can easier be had through Fuller and
Browne, Dryden and Waller, than from Claren-
don alone; and so of any period whose affairs
are supplemented by contemporary writings.
The motives which inspire the outward acts
are oftenest disclosed by the portrayals of the
inward spirit of an age.

In this large-minded method an antidote also
will be found to the microscopic tendency
Prevents narrowness. which a narrower criticism is apt to
produce.　It is far removed from
the petty scrutinising of the lower forms,
and farther still from the hazardous flippancy,
or the snappish censoriousness of the very
lowest.　By it the writings of any age will be
viewed in their proper perspective, and estimated not by their local and temporary values
so much as by their relative and perpetual importance.　Which method it is better to follow
will admit of but one answer from any who
have ambitions beyond disposing of so many
volumes in so many minutes.　Happily men's
ambitions are frequently above the level of
their necessities, and they would take larger
and juster views if they could command the
time which such historical perspective demands.

XIII

CREATIVE CRITICISM

"I criticise by creation, not by finding fault."—MICHEL ANGELO.

AMONG the principles of division applied to the large subject of Literature is the one which separates creative work from critical. This division may not be greatly unequal so far as quantity is concerned, since it places all original production, so called, on one side, and whatever comment on it there may be on the other. Some notion of the smallness of this disparity may be formed by looking through publishers' lists for any year, and also through journals and periodicals for criticisms and notices of their publications. In the aggregate this comment amounts to considerable, especially in the instance of some noteworthy book which may have had as many words printed about it as are contained between its own covers, or

even more.   On the other side there are many
books which get little or no notice, so that the
balance is kept between books and reviews with
something like equality.

As to the relative quality of each kind of
literature it may be averaged as about equal,
considering all the books that are printed of
various degrees of merit, and all that is written
about them with equal variety of judgment.
The common supposition is that it is an easier
task to write about the way an author has
treated a given subject than to make an original
study of it for one's self.   This depends upon
two conditions: first, upon the excellence of
the book produced; second, upon the value of
the criticism about it.   These values may be
interchangeable.   The author may be far above
the critic; or the critic may surpass the author
in his knowledge and even in his treatment of
the topic discussed by both.   As the higher
grades only are to be contemplated here in this
branch of higher criticism, it may be inquired,
if there is not a possible degree of excellence in
comment which approaches the best creative
composition and even crosses the boundary
which is supposed to separate it from the critical.   In other words, may there not be in the
best examples of the literature of judgment as
much originality as in the corresponding grade

of the literature of creation ? A negative answer seems the only one possible when Shakespeare or any other genius is set over against his critics, since commentators have not yet been represented by anything more than pre-eminent talent, except when genius has turned aside to criticise, as in the instance of Goethe. Even when one reads an article on " Tennyson and his Critics " it is expected that the poet will be shown to have the advantage over his judges. Still, there is a place for criticism not far below that supernal sphere occupied by genius. In this most respectable circle there have been intellectual achievements which far outrank much that passes for original work, and deserves far more the appellation Creative. It will bear comparison with what is called first-class composition in other departments of literature, particularly in the field of exposition and the Essay.

The readiest confirmation of this statement is found in the works of eminent critics themselves. Sainte-Beuve, Renan, Taine, Brunetière, in France; Arnold, Bagehot, Saintsbury, Dowden, Gosse, Stephen, Lamb, Macaulay, in England; and before these, the British reviewers of the early part of this century, not to mention our own Lowell, and Poe at his best, with critics now in the field,—all these have done critical work which approaches the best creative, surpassing whole libraries of mediocre originality, original only in the sense of recombination. One writer upon composition has gone so far as to say that, " the highest type of the literary writer is the literary critic." He cites in proof:

"Longinus, in his treatise on the Sublime; Lessing in his dissertations on German Poetry and Greek Art ; Dryden in his studies of classical and vernacular verse ; Sainte-Beuve in his brilliant survey of authors and books . . . writers with regard to whom it would be difficult to say where they have done their greater work, in thought or in æsthetic art." [1]

Some inquiry into the elements and qualities which make critical composition creative may help to establish this position. The first step should be to determine in what sense anything human can be created. The primary definition of " causing something to exist," to which some might add " out of nothing," being set apart as the sole prerogative of Deity, it may be sufficient to apply to human effort the secondary signification of the word, namely, " to invest something with a new character." A discussion might here be

Creative qualities.

---

[1] Professor T. W. Hunt, *Studies in Literature and Style.*

entered upon in regard to an intermediate act of creating thoughts so new that the act shall seem akin to creating a world out of chaos. As this word chaos does not imply a lack of material but only a confusion of it, so the most original conceptions may be nothing more than readjustment of pre-existing ideas. It is fair, then, to limit intellectual creativeness to the act of clothing in new form, investing with new character, and combining in novel arrangement thoughts that have previously existed. If this process be applied to those ideas which are found in any book, and with such felicity as to avoid the imputation and the tiresomeness of repetition, a step toward creative criticism has been taken.

This statement may be made clearer by comparing the old-fashioned commentary on the Scriptures with modern suggestive exposition. Such comment was careful to make Holy Writ understood by substituting later words or phrases for archaisms, and by filling gaps in the sense with extended paraphrase; adding explanations where they were necessary, and oftener where they were not, so that it was sometimes said of such commentaries as their chief commendation, that they were " good in easy places." Every pains seemed to be taken not to add a thought which was not conveyed by the context, perfectly or imperfectly. Such interpretation had its uses, its values, and its virtues. It elucidated the text so far as it was able, but it did nothing more, and left the reader to make such application of it as he might. Beyond this is what may be termed suggestive and creative exposition, showing how widely these tersely stated germ truths reach, and how varied is their application to different ages and conditions of human life in all time and the world over.

Similar qualities prevail in literary criticism, interpretative and creative. The first is useful, is just to the author, and is essential to the second. But the second, as literature, is an advance upon the first, if it is well done, and fulfils the conditions implied in its name, Creative.

What are these conditions ? First that the critic, in some particulars, go beyond the work which the author has performed. Remembering the rights of the author in the matter of fair representation, and being careful not to substitute an opinion of his own as the author's when interpreting him, the critic may suggest other applications of the writer's statements and ideas, theories and facts. Within the ordinary limits imposed upon the reviewer there will not be great opportunity to do this, unless he confine himself to one or two points, or write a larger work on the subject himself—a thing not unknown in the history of controversial criticism. While extended space is not essential to suggestive writing, it will commonly be found that creative criticism belongs to elaborate discussion, and is to be looked for in the works of the masters in this art. Room being allowed the critic, his creative performance will be unhampered. He will feel that he is free to carry the teachings of his text into unoccupied territory.

In such procedure the author's positions will become the critic's starting-point, but his excursions will be limited only by his own ability to traverse the field upon which the author has entered. Like any other explorer he may begin at the last outpost of his predecessor and go as much farther as he can. This is what he would be expected to do if he were writing the latest treatise on any science, as distinguished from a text-book recounting its achievements up to date. He would have no justification for his work, beyond a possibly more attractive presentation of known facts, if he did not add to this new discoveries or thoughts of his own. There is no reason why creative criticism should not do in its way what independent re-

search and fresh discovery do, namely, go
one step farther, or as many steps as it can.
In this way it rises to the dignity of Invention,
as opposed to re-statement and repetition.
It opens up new reaches of vision and discloses
truths towards which an author was drifting or
pointing, blocked, possibly, by obstacles insur-
mountable in the brief polar summer in which
every man must do his best work of discovery
before the long night falls.   Thus Parry's extreme outpost shall become Franklin's starting-
point, whose last flag-staff shall be De Long's
point of departure.   From his last station Mel-
ville shall make a stretch beyond, and Nansen
push still farther forward toward the pole.
Each is the interpreter and developer of the
theories of his predecessor, but each adds new
discoveries by his own explorations.   It is the
same procedure in all the world of mind and
in every department of literature.   If literature
itself is " a criticism of life," there is also life
and growth in the criticism of literature.   Every
worthy branch of it has its quickening, suggestive, and therefore creative power in the mind
which is attentive and receptive, responsive
and aggressive.   It catches inspiration from
the commonest fact when its mood is like the
mountain atmosphere that is charged with St.
Elmo's fire, and upon slight provocation illu-

mines paths before untrodden. Out of old and accepted truths, familiar to men in their triteness of statement, it is the prerogative of the higher criticism to bring new forms and applications; but no less to make the old treasures the capital by which new fields shall be reached and new wealth discovered. Thus it becomes more than exposition and more than interpretation. It becomes creative, inspiring in him who reads aright further exposition and larger creation.

What is here meant can be best understood by a diligent reading of the higher forms of criticism contained in the works of the masters in this department of literature. One will not have to look far in the critical writings of Dryden, Addison, Johnson, Coleridge, Lamb, De Quincey, Carlyle, Arnold, Ruskin, or Lowell to find examples of a creative criticism which has gone beyond what is criticised into the outer ranges of thought.

Take for an example Matthew Arnold's suggestive remarks about translating Homer, extending through three lectures, and some " last words " in a fourth, and turn to the passage showing that the poet did not rise and sink with his subject and was never prosaic and low.

14

" But," the author says, " I never denied that a *subject* must rise and sink, that it must have its elevated and its level regions. . . . What distinguishes the greatest masters of poetry from all others is, that they are perfectly sound and poetical in these level regions of their subject,—in these regions which are the great difficulty of all poets but the very greatest, which they never quite know what to do with. A poet may sink in these regions by being falsely grand as well as by being low. . . . A passage of the simplest narrative is quoted to me from Homer, and I am asked whether Homer does not sink *there ?* My answer is, ' Those lines are very good poetry indeed, poetry of the best class, *in that place.* ' "

After contrasting an attempt of Wordsworth's to not sink in a similar place, and becoming pompous instead of poetical in consequence, he goes on to discuss the meaning of " the grand style," and finally ends with the definition that " the grand style arises in poetry *when a noble nature, poetically gifted, treats with simplicity or with severity a serious subject.*" He then cites Homer as the best model of the grand style, and Milton as the best of the " grand severe," and Dante as affording admirable examples of both styles, simplicity and severity.

In this exposition there is implied a criticism

of translators, and also of his own critics, but he has gone far beyond both in his discernment of principles which they had not surmised, much less defined. He sees the " great personality and noble nature " of the poet in and beyond his verse, and discovers principles toward which translators and commentators had been working their way without perceiving how near they were to a vast, open sea of truth.

This, then, is what is intended here by the term creative criticism: discovery made by pursuing all former researches to their last attainment, and from their remotest standpoint projecting the reasoning, perceptive, and imaginative powers of the intellect like a search-light into the unknown land beyond. Note how Ruskin strides on in his classification of poets:

Ruskin in classification of poets.

" first the men who feel nothing, and therefore see truly ; second, the men who feel strongly, think weakly, and see untruly (second order of poets) ; third, the men who feel strongly, think strongly, and see truly (first order of poets); fourth, the men who, strong as human creatures can be, are yet submitted to influences stronger than they are, and see in a sort untruly, because what they see is inconceivably above them. This last is the usual condition of prophetic inspiration. . . . The difference between the great and less man is, that the first knows too much of the past and future and of all things beside that which immediately affects him to be in any wise shaken by it. His mind is made up; his ways are steadfast. He is tender to impression at the surface, like a rock with deep moss upon it ; but there is too much of him to be moved. The smaller man is carried off his feet. . . . He is gay and enthusiastic, melancholy and passionate and as things come and go with him. Therefore the high creative poet might be thought impassive (as shallow people think Dante stern)."

In this way he goes on to characterise the moods of different orders of poets according to principles which he is laying down as new, or at least as a new version and fulfilment of the old law. Thus he arrives at his final definition of consummate poetical temperament :

"The greatness of a poet depends upon the two faculties, acuteness of feeling, and command of it . . . there being always a point beyond which it would be inhuman if he pushed this control, and, therefore, a point at which all wild fancy becomes just and true. It overthrows the prophet of Israel when he contemplates the destruction of Assyria."

As a final example of creative criticism turn to Lowell's "Shakespeare Once More." Lamb,

Hazlitt, Coleridge, and Arnold had uttered their last word, and hundreds of lesser writers had followed them implicitly or dif-   Lowell on
fered from their conclusions.   Then Shakespeare.
Lowell took up the " most rhythmic genius, acutest intellect, profoundest imagination, and healthiest understanding of the race " in connection with some of his higher achievements. He pays a compliment to the researches of Goethe and Lessing, Schlegel and Gervinus, and then honestly adds:

" With the help of all these, and especially the last, I shall apply this theory of criticism to Hamlet, not in the hope of saying anything new, but to support the thesis . . . that his higher object was to create something which should deserve to be called a work of art. Supposing him to have accepted the new terms of the problem which makes character the pivot of dramatic action, and consequently the key to dramatic unity, how far did he succeed ? "

The very statement of this proposition carries the reader a long reach into the forefront of dramatic criticism, and augurs a survey of unexplored territory.   He prefaces this outlook with a sentence which a topographical engineer might have spoken: " Before attempting my analysis, I must clear away a little rubbish." Then brushing aside Voltaire's accusation of anachronisms, and the objection to comic scenes in tragedy, he addresses himself to what may be called a most consummate exhibition of advanced criticism.

Taking the character of Hamlet as the germ of the play, Lowell speaks of its " genealogical necessity," a mixture of the father's infirmity of will and the mother's persistence; the son's consciousness of this defect; Horatio's continuity of character as a foil to Hamlet's unsteadiness; the hitherto neglected element of inclination to irony in Hamlet, unlike Timon's or Iago's. Then he passes to the much discussed question of Hamlet's madness, not in relation to the case as others have considered it, but respecting the *character* in its completeness. After this comes his conception of the scope of the higher drama:

" to represent life by nobler reaches of language and the inspiring influence of verse and intenser play of passion, condensing the ordinary atmosphere of existence into flashes of thought and phrase, printing the outworn landscape of every day upon our brains in lines of tell-tale fire."

In the rapid disclosure of the central motives in Lear, Macbeth, and Othello as teaching the lessons of tragedy and, by indirection, the ethics of life; his discernment that the higher things than those which come by plot and observation may be unconsciously written by the original poet; and finally the moral that he draws from Hamlet, that Will is Fate, and Will, once abdicating, gives place to Chance on the throne,—all this and more that he says in the intense suggestiveness of his own inspiring words marks the critic in the teeming processes of creation far afield, as distinguished from the plodding commentator turning the sod which his predecessors have turned for a dozen generations.

If anyone supposes that the literature which is written about literature must of necessity be uninspiring and unsuggestive because it works on lines laid down by another author, let him read the discoveries and propositions which great critics like the three here mentioned have made as they took long strides beyond the latest explorer. The last word, however, has not been said, and untrodden territory still lies beyond, as the encircling ocean-stream to the ancients flowed beyond and around all their lands.

Therefore there still remain to criticism fields for its highest endeavor and its best achievement. As literature in its various branches enlarges and grows better and richer, its outlying margin of the unattained will lie as open to the critic as to the author; and no one can foretell which, in any year, will pre-empt the most of unclaimed regions and develop their hid treasures. The author may have the advantage of special study and investigation; but the critic may appropriate all his discoveries in a month, and in the next set his stakes and pitch his tent on remoter acres beyond.

XIV

THE VALUE OF CRITICISM TO
LITERATURE

" We chat together; he gives me his prescriptions ; I never follow them, and so get well."—MOLIÈRE.

THIS practical age is always asking what a thing is worth. It has its opinion about literature and the value of its several departments. In regard to criticism as one of them, its inquiry is respecting its service to literature in general. For it cannot be denied that in some ages and some countries it has been customary to regard criticism as a parasite subsisting upon literature rather than serving it or supporting an independent life of its own. Possibly such a view of it still prevails here and there. How correct it may be depends upon the nature of the criticism contemplated and many other considerations, whose number and diversity tend to produce great difference of opinion in

217

this as in other matters pertaining to the art. Doubtless there is something that often passes for criticism which is nothing more than a restatement of the substance of a book, or a part of it. While such treatment has its value to the public, it cannot be regarded as judgment or independent comment. On the other hand, if criticism becomes anything more than an abstract or digest, it begins to be more than a parasite, and to derive its life from the soil instead of from the tree. It becomes a vine instead of a fungus. The vine may grow about the tree, but it has a life of its own which must find its expression and expansion in some direction. So the book may become a trellis to genuine criticism, sometimes a very slight one. To originality it need be no more a contributor than the dead tree is to the creeper which overruns and adorns it. Accordingly the charge of being parasitic depends for its validity on the kind of criticism. Even if it is a parasite it may have a service to perform for literature that cannot well be spared. Mosses may serve to indicate decay; the puff-ball, poverty of soil. Both these may have their counterparts in critical literature with corresponding uses.

It is, however, another kind of criticism and *Restrictive value.* its different service to letters that now demands attention. In general

this includes all interpretative and creative comment and discussion, and does not exclude
restrictive and destructive estimates.   Perhaps
its most obvious service lies in these last offices
of limitation and exclusion.   Did anyone ever
contemplate without a shudder the amount of
literature, so called, that would flood the earth
if book-making were as feasible as book-writing?
As it is, the printer and binder and paper
manufacturer, and the publisher representing
them, stand between the public and the multitude of writers as a sort of breakwater.   Nevertheless, in spite of barriers, there is a steady
flow of volumes rolling over the land in a constantly increasing tide.   The publisher's readers
and advisers are the critics whose judgment
avails most to regulate the supply of literature,
in accordance with the demand for it in every
department.   All subsequent criticism is retro-
active, so far as first editions are concerned;
while the publisher's critics determine the
question whether or not manuscripts shall be
printed.   They do not publish their estimates
in the newspapers; they do not add their own
comments, nor indulge in comparative, interpretative, or creative criticism in periodicals
and in books of their own, as a rule; but as a
class of critics their service to the reading public is in inverse proportion to the publicity of

their work and in direct ratio to its silence and secrecy. They are the unseen registration officers passing upon the credentials of every applicant for citizenship in the community of letters and membership in the brotherhood of authors. If their opinion in severalty or in the aggregate could be had, as that of later critics is obtained from the press, it would be of inestimable value to writers. It is to be deplored that each aspirant to authorship cannot afford the services of such an adviser. The commonwealth of readers would do itself a service to maintain a board of discreet counsellors for the encouragement or discouragement of beginners, in fiction especially, and in other branches of composition as well. As Irving remarks of critics in general, they would be '' a salutary check on the over-production of literature, like those on population. By all means let critics be encouraged, good and bad, lest the world be swamped with books.'' All honor, then, to the invisible bench of judges who stop four manuscripts out of five on their way to the public library, the reading-room, and the fireside. In fact, the calculation has been made that this number is as high as nine out of ten. Writers are disappointed, to be sure, but it is not to many of them a matter of deprivation or starvation. Life is more than letters, and there are plenty of abandoned farms which will afford many writers a larger pittance than the pen. It is safe to say, that the income from books that are published in most cases adds little to an author's competence, or else, in rare instances, makes his fortune—generally by a lucky hit in the direction of a text-book or a novel.

In the multiplicity of books which are published on account of a real or supposed demand by the public, there is, then, this **Regulative.** regulative service for criticism to perform in behalf of good literature. The most obvious feature of it to some would seem to be still further restriction by adverse comment; to others, enlargement by commendation. There may be so much of both in any instance as to neutralise the influence of each; but the intent of the critic must be taken for what it is worth, and the value of criticism for what it accomplishes. In the case of a bad or worthless book, the weight of remark will be against it and usually affect its sale and circulation. A prominent journal remarks most pertinently, that

" it is often asked what good the critics do. In some cases they have put an end to the booklets and bardlets of the Decadence—improper books which their writers called 'the independent in literature and the individual' not based upon the Decalogue.''

A good and useful book will as surely be advertised as such by a large proportion of reviewers who are discriminating and fair in their judgment and its avowal. Sometimes sales have been increased by unfavourable reviews,[1] as in the case of Froude, who was helped rather than hurt by the dead set made against him in certain critical quarters. For the commonalty of readers, then, the influence of a book is restricted or enlarged by judicious comment. In general this itself is affected consciously or unconsciously by the sentiment of the leaders of opinion. More or less it is the answer which public taste returns to the publisher's reader concerning a book which he has allowed to appear before the populace for its suffrages. Between both kinds of critics the service rendered thus far is to literature through the consumers of it and its patrons the buyers.

The makers of literature must also be considered. What services is criticism rendering to authors ? This is one of the vexed questions between critics and writers. It would be possible to conduct a debate on

Service to authors.

---

[1] *Authors and Publishers*, p. 55.

paper with citations of opinion from both parties. The traditional antagonism between author and critic would be exemplified by such quotations. Now and then some arbiter between them asserts that this opposition is superficial, the one being the helper of the other, or his expounder. This, however, is a position maintained chiefly by the critics, but one which authors also might take with equal honesty and grace. One of them has said for his guild, that " to a young author criticism shows where he is weak and sometimes where he is strong, and that he may learn much from it if he does not allow adverse notices to depress and dishearten him. The difficulty is that hardly any two critics agree." Against this may be placed the following from " a novelist of experience," who remarks that

" such an one has nothing to learn from a young gentleman fresh from Oxford or Cambridge who is just as qualified to lecture him on his ignorance of the canons of art as he is to denounce a Chancellor of the Exchequer about his knowledge of the first principles of taxation. Yet I cannot blame these young critics, for I remember my own escapades in that direction." [1]

Another, speaking of Matthew Arnold, says

[1] Wm. Black

that " he helped his countrymen to distinguish the good from the bad, the noble from the ignoble, the ephemeral from the enduring in what they read." The inference from this is: a beneficial reaction upon writers through an improved taste in the public mind. This, doubtless, is more effective than direct attack upon authors themselves, or than advice which is easier given than followed.

One of the stock arguments against the value of criticism to literature is, that the ancient *Objections to repressive criticism.* classics were produced in ages when critics did not exist. Or, that in modern times the last thing which great and original writers have had in view as they wrote was the critic standing ready to swoop down upon their finished product and tear it in pieces. The first of these statements is easier to imagine true than the second. A careless freedom may be observed in the early literatures of all nations which cannot be reconciled with the presence of an intimidating criticism. On the other hand, later writers have not always stood in so much awe of it as they might for their profit. Yet no one is warranted in saying that every distinguished writer is entirely oblivious to whatever may be showered upon him; or that having the fear of the judge before his eyes he may not write more carefully than if there were no inspector to report upon his work. Still, he would be sadly repressed in his freedom of composition if he should ask at every turn, What will the critics say to this ? Considering their number and their variations of taste and judgment, he might better ask, What may they not say ? Perhaps the sentence or page he is writing may be condemned by the purist. If he strike it out, the Johnsonian will say that something is lacking. If he take extreme positions, he will be a radical to one; if he take moderate views, he will be accused of indifference and double-mindedness by another. The very diversity of criticism will thus breed despairing heedlessness of it in the first edition. Comment may modify a second, and induce revision; but it can have little more effect upon the first than respect for the opinion of readers has.

Criticism, then, as a formative influence upon literature, operates slowly and retroactively through emendation of what has been done without securing much regard for itself in the writer's first effort. With all his faults of freedom, there would be more if he always kept an eye upon his waiting accuser. For in every composition that has been worth great attention every line has been pounced upon by some Stymphalian bird, if for no better reason, because the rest of the flock had overlooked it. Such at least has been the fate of annotated classics in all languages. The note may be of admiration or of censure, but it is critical. Suppose that Homer could have looked down the long vista of centuries to see keen eyes and sharp beaks awaiting his passing to the end of time, would there have been the breezy freedom in his verse that suggests the inspiration of waves and winds and the battles and speech of unaffected, majestic men ? Or if he could come back after sixty generations and wade through the commentators from Aristarchus and Zoilus to the last German folio on the Homeric use of $\delta\acute{\epsilon}$ or some other particle, would he write a revised and improved edition of the *Iliad?* Would Spenser's exuberant phantasy, like his gentle knight, have " pricked so gaily o'er the plain " if he had seen the thorny caltrops which were to be sown along his course ? Would Shakespeare's pen have halted when it was writing " a little more than kin, and less than kind " if he could have seen the clans putting their heads together to determine what he meant, and could have witnessed their scrimmages over the question ? Very likely he would have made this and some other passages clearer, but if he had heeded every suggestion of his critics what kind of a Hamlet and Othello and Lear would have been created, or, rather, how many kinds ?

On the whole, perhaps, it is well for our best literature that criticism of it must be post-natal. Prevision and dread apprehension of critical judgment certainly cannot be inspiring to creative processes. If Aristotle had known that he would be accused of ignorance, Virgil of a want of invention, Horace of obscurity, Cicero of a lack of vigour, Demosthenes of want of purity in language, as they all were accused, and of other faults besides, would their virtues of composition have lost anything through the fear that these too might be censured in the wide distribution of blame ? If Shakespeare had foreseen that Rymer, whom Pope esteemed a great critic, would say, " His brains are turned; he raves and rambles without coherence "; and that Lansdowne and Voltaire and Edwards would speak no better of his rhyme or reason; that Theobald and Pope would not esteem him too highly, nor any critics in England until German scholars had touched British eyes and made them see; would the great Elizabethan dramatist and his fellows have left so priceless an inheritance as they did leave ? If they could also have seen the relative value of their own productive age and that of the critical ones which followed, and the relative importance of Shakespeare and Dryden, of Ben Jonson and Samuel Johnson, of Marlowe and Pope, it is possible that they might have said, Let us go to and build, trusting the judgment of our work to ages beyond the classic or romantic.

Milton appears to have had faith in the future more than in a generation which would give only five pounds for *Paradise Lost*, and he does not appear to have allowed contemporary criticism to greatly disturb his muse. He was not the sort of man to change a line even if he had foreseen that Doctor Johnson would speak slightingly of his verse. Still, it would be interesting to know if contemporary critics were responsible in any measure for the inferiority of *Paradise Regained*. Meantime Warton and Salmasius are remembered only because they were Milton's critics.

The literary judges of his time were prompt enough in Wordsworth's case to affect his production, and severe enough to suppress it, and him too if he could have been suppressed. Such treatment might well account for sundry flaws in the verse of some of the Lake Poets. Much of their inspiration must have been derived from the slings and arrows of outrageous criticism. How much better their work would have been without such stimulus must be left to authors and critics to discuss.

A half century ago a review-writer remarked that '' it is questionable whether the criticism of the British Reviews on contemporaries was not, on the whole, productive of evil.'' Another asserted that

'' Criticism can never be prospective until the resources of man and of nature are exhausted. Even in our own time we can trace the complete abolition of popular rules of criticism by the new and unexpected combinations of genius.   If the old maxim that no interesting fiction can be grafted on history were still in force, where would the Waverley novels have been ? ''

Still another observes that

'' much of the narrowness and captiousness which we observe in ludicrous connection with some of the noblest thoughts and most exalted imaginations of the poets of the present century, had their source in the stings which vindictive and flippant reviewers had planted in their minds.''

One other goes so far as to

'' doubt whether either writer or reader is benefited by what is commonly called criticism.   The former is rendered cautious and distrustful ; he fears to give way to those kindling emotions and brave sallies of thought which bear him up to excellence ; the latter is made fastidious and cynical, surrendering his own independent taste and judgment and learns to like and dislike at second hand. They grow timorous in judgment, since that of critics themselves is often reversed.''

It must be granted to this side of the discussion that criticism is not likely to be anticipatory in the benefits it confers on the makers of literature. They must be free to do their work without much repression or much direction even. Their product may be good or bad, but experience shows that it will not be much bettered by the fear of strictures upon it. Cervantes, Tasso, Racine, and Keats were not improved by the contemporary criticism that pursued them. It naturally antagonised them against all its possible benefits. All such might say with *Milverton :*[1] '' I go on never minding; and when I am particularly attacked I exclaim with Spinster Strachey, ' Perhaps the good gentlemen would agree with me if they knew this parish as well as I do.' '' So difficult is it for criticism to adopt the '' alongside canon '' with reference to the writer when he is writing. And the

Benefits of criticism not anticipatory.

[1] In *Friends in Council.*

author, perplexed by different opinions, goes his own way, or, timorous through too much regard for what the next verdict will be, lets his pen fall in despair and discouragement.

If there were no other side to this discussion there would seem to be no good answer to the question in substance of a modern critic[1]—Are critics of any use in literature ? and of what use ? Several replies have been made to such inquiries. Eighty-seven years ago one of the fraternity grandly declared, " We profess the stately office of correcting and instructing." Accepting the validity of the claim, it must be concluded that the instruction is by means of correction, and therefore, as remarked above, *ex post facto* in its method, so far as any one work is concerned and the author of it. Yet such instructive correction, or corrective instruction, may have a value for other writers, and thus for literature in general and classes of it in particular. That is, the author of a history or a novel who has failed in some important requisite of historical or novel writing, if made an example of, furnishes instruction through his censor to other writers of similar books. Thus criticism contributes to the elevation of literature by a retrospective process. Of course this

Corrective value.

[1] W. D. Howells.

implies careful observation of current criticism on the part of the makers of literature. Human frailty helps in this study by its easy impressibility as to the mistakes of others, which, in other directions, constitute almost as large a part of education as one's own mistakes. Besides, authors are uncommonly observant of other men's ventures in their own departments. One can imagine the interest with which Motley read reviews of Prescott's histories on a subject akin to his own, the domination of Spain, and *vice versa*. The great army of novelists to-day must find much instruction in the numerous reviews of contemporary work that are published every day and every week. It is certainly possible for them to get clear notions of the tendency of the time and its demands upon writers of fiction. Now and then they have an opportunity to learn by the unanimity of critical approval what has made a story immensely successful, or by disapproval what has made it a failure. Profiting by this information, it would be strange if the makers of fiction did not in the aggregate improve its character year by year; or if not improved by them, it will at least be conformed to the changes in popular taste and standards. Thus the critic reaches the writer through his criticism of other writers; and all the more effectively because he has lashed him over other men's shoulders, or praised his method as practised by someone else, without the risk of turning the author's head with direct laudation. This is one of the services criticism renders literature—by educating its creators.

Another service is in its incidental education of readers. It is for them ostensibly that reviews of books are written. They read them openly, and accept what they read with what must seem to the critic a delightful credulity. [*Instruction of readers.*] They do not take his strictures into a dark corner to peruse with chagrin and unprofitable wrath, as authors do, —provided they reverence the critic. Instead, they open their minds to his comments, and let his impressions of a new book sink even more deeply into their spirits, because they have no counteracting impressions of their own, not having read the volume themselves, or else having run rapidly and unreflectingly through it. What more favourable conditions for education can be imagined? The spirit of docility itself could not be more perfectly illustrated. In consequence, the critic makes rapid progress in forming the literary taste of such readers, provided they have the capacity to appreciate his instruction and its standards. Soon his views help to make that consensus of opinion which controls the market, and regulates the demand and finally the supply in literature. Thus the author is reached by the most effective of methods—the possibility or impossibility of publishing what he has to say. The taste of the community is educated meantime, and the cause of letters served by general criticism—that is, if it is reasonably consistent with itself in its main principles and standards. If it is not, credulity is shaken by disagreements, dissensions, and opposing judgments, and beautiful confidence is succeeded by skittish distrust. After all, the French critic may be right who says that " the public learns to accept criticism for what it is worth, caring neither for the laurels it bestows nor for the vials of wrath it pours out." [1]

In corroboration of these positions, a few authorities may be profitably cited. With regard to the general question of criticism as a help to production, Lowell wrote:

Citation of opinions.

" Fixed principles of criticism are useful in helping us to form a judgment of works already produced, but it is questionable whether they are not a hindrance rather than a help to living production. . . . A constant reference to the statutes which taste has codified would only bewilder the creative

[1] M. Caro.

instinct.   Criticism can at best teach writers without genius what is to be avoided or imitated."[1]

Mr. Howells agrees with this opinion so far as to say, in substance, that criticism cannot affect the performance of a writer, but only the esteem in which he is held by the public.   A recent writer in *Blackwood*, while disclaiming the idea that an author is mainly something for the critic to exhibit his own wit upon, considers it " the main if not the sole province of the reviewer to show the way in which the writer has done his work; and this for the benefit of the general congregation of decently educated and intelligent people."   Still stronger ground is taken by a writer in the *Atlantic Monthly* who holds that " sound criticism is an indispensable basis for the development of a great national literature." And another: " The critical power, though on a distinctly lower level than the creative, is of inestimable help in its development."   Opposed to this is the opinion of a writer on criticism in general and John Dennis in particular, who is perhaps so much influenced by contemplating the methods of Dennis that he remarks:

" It is evident that the art of criticism is not requi-

[1] *Essays*, ii., 222.

site to the development of genius, because in all the golden ages of poetry it has had no portion, nor even constructed the scaffolding to aid in the erection of the cloud-capped towers and solemn temples of the bard.''

Despite these differences of opinion, any honest author will admit that fair criticism has been of considerable service to him. It has the same value to a writer that one watching a game may have to those playing it. A spectator outside the contest sees some things which must escape the participant in it. The absorbing eagerness with which a thinker may be pursuing one line of thought may make him oblivious to some other of equal value to which the critic may call his attention. This the critic may be permitted to do while admitting that the subject in hand cannot be exhausted in a single treatise. The value of such suggestion, however made, is often seen in revised editions of important works, and is frequently acknowledged in a prefatory note. Reduced to its final terms, the traditionary hostility between authors and critics would disappear entirely if there were always conscientious competence on the one side and admission of the fallibility which is only human, on the other. Lord Ellenborough and Sir Alexander Cock-

Value of criticism to authors to be admitted.

burn's statement of an author's risks ought to open his eyes to what he may expect to incur. The last says, and the first agrees with him: " Every man who publishes a book commits himself to the judgment of the public, and anyone may comment upon his performance." Therefore upon the appearance of his book he needs to don a thick jacket, and, as the knights of the camera suggest to their victims, " to assume a pleasant expression." He must also remember that he has had his first word, and that the last one belongs to the critic. All attempts of an author to have the last one himself are vain. He may ask for information and find a genial gentleman with no name who will give it; but he will not expect to correspond with him in print, in order to correct him. " If a fellow attacked my opinions in print would I reply ? " asks the Autocrat of the Breakfast Table. " Not I. . . . Controversy equalises fools and wise men in the same way—and the fools know it." The genial Doctor must have had one of the minor critics in mind, like " the young fellow called John," whom he snubbed so often.

There is one means of redress which an author may at least attempt to employ—with what satisfaction he will be able to decide after he has made the attempt

Author-critics.

—that is, to turn critic himself. Walter Savage Landor is one of several who have said with sourness, that " all critics are but authors who have failed."   Those who are such failures will be apt to find in critical writing one more opportunity to fail.   Possibly this is their Bonanza vein of ability hitherto undiscovered, but probably not.   The chances are against them.   Criticism of the best sort may not be the most valuable find in literature, but it is as rare as aluminum used to be,—and all inferior kinds as common and cheap as that metal now is.   Nevertheless Hall Caine says that,

" according to the periodical press of our own time, criticism is a sort of tourney in which critics and authors may be both combatants and judges ; in which a man may first disport himself in the lists, and afterward mount the dais and forthwith adjudicate on his rivals."

This seems the only dignified way to adjust difficulties and preserve equilibrium.   The author will thus incidentally be likely to take juster views of the value of criticism to literature, himself now being both critic and judge. He will also find how difficult a task it is to read a book in the spirit and from the point of view of the writer; to be just to him while differing from him ; to so interpret his message to readers that they shall get the gist of it and the best of it, thus serving the interests of literature in general by the good offices of this auxiliary branch in particular.

XV

SERVICES OF CRITICISM TO ITSELF

" Happy are they that can hear their detractions and can put them to mending."—SHAKESPEARE.

SINCE criticism is of undoubted service to literature of all other kinds, it would be singular if it should be found to have no value to itself as an important department of letters.

As a department of literature. Apart from the accepted law whereby no one greatly benefits others without incidental and reflex advantage to himself, it may be asked, In what ways have critics been of service to their art, and by complying with what methods may they be of even greater service as one generation of them succeeds another ?

Primarily it may be said that the best service to any art depends upon exalted views concerning it on the part of those who practise it. No man can do effective work who does not believe in the worth of his vocation. If a critic entertain a low estimate of criticism, regarding it as a petty censorship, or as furnishing chances to display one's self at another's expense, or as a mere bread-winning drudgery, he will do little for the advancement of his profession.

Such views were better dropped at once in all consideration of things that are valuable to criticism as an art, science, or literature. Instead, it may be more profitable to gather some testimony to a higher and better conception of the nature and purpose of criticism as expressed by its best advocates. For in this way they have rendered at least a primary service to their art.

Such inquiry naturally starts with definitive statements by one and another of what criticism is and is not. A complete view of the subject cannot, of course, be contained in one sentence or two; but it can be readily determined

whether such a view indicates a high or low estimate of the art. When, for instance, Voltaire said that "an excellent critic should have much science and taste, without prejudice and without envy," it is plain that he made a comprehensive statement, containing positive and negative qualifications of a critic, and implying a dignified conception of his office. A severer idea of it is manifested by Diderot's reply to Sedaine when the poet suggested that there was feeling and soul in his criticism: " You poets," he answered, " employ feeling in writing of love and in creating terrible or charming beings; but I, when I put my heart into my judgments, act as a poor surgeon does who cuts and bleeds with a feeling which wastes itself upon the sick in a grievous and unfruitful manner."   This is not precisely the view taken by those who are cut and bled by criticism, but it may be the correct one when the cause of sound literature is considered.   There is, however, a difference between surgery and slashing, which the critic will always bear in mind.

Some thirty-five years ago there was a general sense of the better way in France, according to M. Caro, when a book on its appearance

"became the object of careful and scrupulous examination.   It was deeply studied, well weighed, and judged on its merits.   .   .   .   The public had competent guides to direct its choice.   In those happy days the critics were recognised oracles of good sense, reason, and sound knowledge.   They set the current of opinion about new works, made and explained success or failure.   They were not always infallible, nor even impartial ; but at any rate they were seldom far mistaken."

Here was a period, then, in the history of criticism in France which by its work elevated the standard above what it had been, and according to M. Caro, above what it now is. For he adds, that " while there are still good critics in France the influence of some is recognised within a small sphere only, and the talents of others are employed in the field of politics." Nevertheless, both by the many in the former age and by the few survivors in the present, much has been done for the service of the art by the lofty conception of it which critics held and maintained.

The same is true of the later critics in England, especially as contrasted with their predecessors. · Sixty years ago a writer expressed the opinion of readers, if not of critics, when he wrote: " As a general rule (for there are honourable exceptions), they whose business it is to *do* Criticism seem really not to be aware of the dignity and importance of their vocation."   He complains of its being shuffled off on apprentices and the unqualified.

In addition to this indifference he might have mentioned the degradation to which it was subjected by unscrupulous, narrow-minded, and virulent practitioners whose abilities were great, but whose dispositions were spoiled by partisanship.   With the entry of the last third of the century a better sentiment and higher estimate began to be rife in England and America.   Deliverance came in some of Macaulay's work, notwithstanding his occasional indulgence in traditional asperities.   He dealt largely with the greater qualities and prominent features of an author, rather than with minor faults and superficial adornments.   Like Emerson in this respect he valued the solid meaning of thought above the subtler significance of style, a doctrine to which Carlyle also subscribed, so far as he ever subscribed to anything which he was not the first to promulgate. Arnold, on the other hand, goes a step further, considering it the main function of a true critic, " first to know, and then to set up a high standard of literary style and finish, and to judge all books by that standard "; and once more, " to detect and expose insincerity, vulgarity, and the slovenly and pretentious use of words and phrases which are only half understood."   He marks the advance that was made from the first quarter of the century in his rebuke of Wordsworth for taking a low view of criticism, and insists that the critic is one who " has the faculty of judging with all the powers of his mind and soul at work together."   His purpose must be to see the object really as it is, in a spirit of justness.

Perception of the real meaning of facts, of what is the best originality of a writer, and, above all, to " ascertain the master current in the literature of an epoch "—these he regarded as some of the high functions of a true critic. Such views have not been without their value to critics who have followed him, and to contemporaries who caught the contagion of his better spirit, without imitating his dogmatism. As a consequence his service to the art has been great, interpreting as he did a similar movement in French criticism in a day when direct access to its literature was not so feasible as at present.

Other men and other influences have contributed to this elevation of motives and methods of criticism, and thus to its increased value in the domain of letters. The influences are, for the most part, a direct outcome of the high view of the art which has been supplanting the low and narrow sentiments about it which once prevailed. Chief among the exalting agencies is the decline of dogmatism. The older critics cherished high enough conceits of their art on its personal side. They magnified themselves, and their office through their own importance, after the manner of many functionaries. They deemed themselves the incarnation of sound judgment and good taste.   Still, criticism was not advanced as it should have been by such loftiness of sentiment.   If those who entertained it ever wondered why this was so, the reason was not far to find.   One needed to go no farther than the general truth that in literary judgments no one authority is final.   Personal views can contribute in a limited measure to the ruling opinion of an age, but nothing more.   As early as Coleridge's day it had come to be recognised, by him at least, that there must be a code of literary laws as a basis of just criticism, as distinguished from the arbitrary decisions of even great critics.   This was his advanced view,—when he did not happen to have before him a writer who differed from his philosophical or political creed.   On such occasions he too easily fell back into the severity and hostility of his time toward differences in opinion.   But more and more the men who are worthy to be counted his successors in British criticism have been getting out of the ruts in which it is so easy to fall.   The new highway is broader, smoother, and cleaner.   It may not be so amusing to travel, certainly it is not so agitating; but it brings one farther on, with greater ease and speed, and the friction can well be spared, especially if it should be of the kind indicated by such a pronouncement as the following:

" 'The poetry of Mr. Leigh Hunt is such as might be expected from the personal character and habits of its author. As a vulgar man is perpetually labouring to be genteel, in like manner the poetry of this man is always on the stretch to be grand. He is the ideal of a Cockney poet, to whom the one word to be applied is—*Fool!*"

The departure which Coleridge inaugurated in his better mood has been made wider and wider by the generations that followed him. Dropping both dogmatism and splenetic personalities, modern criticism has assumed instead modesty for itself and reasonableness toward the criticised. The diffusion of intelligence, the extension of learning, the multiplication of thoughtful readers, and the spread of a catholic spirit have made imperiousness in judgment out of date. It is gone with the shaggy terror of the full-bottomed wig on the bench. If it roars at all it is the roar of Bottom and of his dove and nightingale. This modesty, moreover, resembles that of genuine learning. It sees that there is little in this world which is absolutely and unqualifiedly certain; that there is no monopoly of truth in any single department of it ; that one spectator cannot encompass a cathedral on all sides at once; that the sun

itself enlightens but one side of the globe at a
time.   Thus the limitation of the human intellect is emphasised by every new expanse of
knowledge, and critics, like astronomers, grow
reverent and modest with each enlargement of
their vision.   Political or philosophical or religious prejudice no longer blinds them to the
achievements of others; and this is not without
its humbling effect which formerly was lost upon
an arrogance that was judicially near-sighted.

A note of this modesty is discernible in the
changed tone of criticism and its altered style.
Two examples may indicate the improvement in fifty years.   " Lord
Byron has improved marvellously
since his last appearance at our tribunal: and
this volume not only atones for the evil work
of his nonage but gives promise of a further
excellence hereafter; to which it is quite comfortable to look forward."   The writer of that
pompous patronage in the *Edinburgh Review*
must have been surveying Auld Reekie and
the rest of Great Britain from the topmost
turret of the castle on the hill with a self-
complacency surpassed only by his self-conceit.
Half a century later Mr. Arnold, who did not
lack confidence in himself, wrote: " Look at
Byron — the greatest natural force and the
greatest elementary power, I cannot but think,

which has appeared in our literature since Shakespeare, . . . who shattered himself to pieces against the precipice of British Philistinism. But Byron, it may be said, was eminent only by his genius," etc.—a proposition which he stops to argue, instead of to assert dogmatically, just as he had already made a qualification in " I cannot but think " in the first sentence quoted above. Dozens of paragraphs might be cited almost at random illustrating the comparative modesty and generosity of recent criticism. The same passages would also exhibit an equal advance in fine discrimination and profound judgment. Brutality and egotism and prejudice blunted many of these perceptive faculties in the moss-trooper age. Even Macaulay and Landor did not escape unharmed. To-day one would have to search long to find a note of dogmatism or superciliousness in the pages of the best contemporary criticism. The presence of such a note would indicate that the criticism containing it is not the best.

Whatever dogmatic individualism was to the age when it flourished, it is certain that the new temper of reserve in declaring Charity and catholicity. opinions, and charity in forming judgments is more consonant with the spirit of our time. Such a mood does much to remove the stigma that had been fastened upon the critical art, and to commend it to the lovers of a thoughtful literature. Serving the reading public by its best methods it has also done itself a service. For if " the highest literary court in criticism is the consensus of educated opinion, assigning their places to writers," then critics, of all men, must conform to those principles which commend any literary work to the good graces of this reading republic.

It would seem sometimes to be forgotten what a large and respectable body the readers of criticism constitute. They are not, to be sure, all the readers of newspapers, or even of magazines and reviews. For this very reason their intelligence, appreciation, and discrimination may compensate for their numerical minority. This is not relatively so small as it often seems. The question, " Have you read such or such a book ? " often brings out the common answer, " No, but I have seen a notice, or read a review of it." This reply comes from the classes in the community who read newspapers for something more than news. They are made up of intelligent, educated, and cultivated persons, using these terms in their commonly accepted meaning and without assigning exact limits or boundaries. They have acquired tastes for books of information in addition to the almost universal love of the story, short and long.   All of them have received at least the modicum of instruction provided at public expense; some are educated, others learned, but all are more or less eager to hear of any new contribution to the stock of human knowledge.   It is not the professional classes alone in this great body of intelligent readers that are interested in even professional books; while those of a general character are sought by all readers.   To many of these the most interesting column of their paper or magazine is not last night's murder, or this morning's runaway, or what bill passed the House yesterday to be defeated in the Senate to-morrow, the remembrance of them all to vanish with the morning mist by noon.   Instead, attention is caught by the titles in the book-column, and interest is kept alive by the notice or abstract, the comment or review of the latest arrivals in the field of letters.   One is interested in a volume of history, another in a scientific treatise, or book upon travel, art, language, literature, a poem, a novel, and some in all these together in varying degree.   It is the only section of their journal which they read from end to end.   For this is the column that brings news from the wide world of mind which is evolving out of its vastness new spheres of thought, small and great, dull and brilliant, but none without their value as indicators of the direction and tendency of humanity and the humanities. Legislation, the price of stocks, the frequency of burglaries may also indicate the drift and rate of national and racial progress, but if one wants to know how far the head of the column has advanced let him look for the latest literature in the newest books, and also observe in what direction it is moving.

To point this out is the privilege of criticism. It is also its grand opportunity to do itself valuable service. In proportion as it is a trustworthy index of the currents which productive literature is creating will it be useful to intelligent communities, and serve itself by increasing the demand for its own good offices. Readers have judgments of their own, and also their preferences and their prejudices; but these are not beyond the influence of better judgment, wiser preference, and prejudice less narrow than their own.

Trustworthiness its recommendation.

Meantime criticism has the chance to create a taste not only for the best literature, but also for itself as a form of it. The subjects it handles are as diversified as the departments of composition and the bent of countless writers. Each may give

Creating a taste for criticism.

a contrasting colour or at least a different shade to every critical composition in those departments and about individual authors. The critic will be blamed no more than a fish for taking the tint of the water he swims in for any hour. This very diversity is a feature of critical literature which gives it relief from the monotony that befalls other writing at times and is tedious to many readers. Or if the critique be long, perhaps to the length of a chapter or a volume, it need not on that account be dull reading. A book about a book may be as good or better than a second volume on the subject by the first author. Reviewing may be an improvement upon coöperation, as in the coöperated novel, for instance, where the chief advantage is in mutual criticism by the authors while writing, thus forestalling some outside strictures. All sides of a subject are more likely to be presented by the critic succeeding to the labours of the author. He has his own allowance of time and space, of perception and expression. It is a poor topic which cannot be treated by two better than by one, and by one following the work of the other. The critic has accordingly a fair field for the cultivation of a superior grade of literary product. He enters into other men's labours. Their harvest becomes his seed for broader sowing. He may improve the seed-grain itself.

That there is a widespread taste and increasing demand for critical composition is evident from the multiplicity of it in journalistic publications. The Review or its predecessors have been running for about two hundred and thirty years. The descendants of the first one, published in 1665, constitute an immense family. Count them in a late number of such a summary as *The Review of Reviews*. They are not, to be sure, all of them, devoted to criticism, but very few are without their reviewing department, and criticism of one kind or another fills a large section in many periodicals and in serial literature itself. It would not if it were not wanted. Editors who are successful know first of all what people wish to read. Readers themselves have ways of making their wants known, generally through the subscription list, the news-vender, and the counting-room at last. They are not backward in giving editors a piece of their mind, anonymously if they can, otherwise if anonymity is not practicable. Between editor and reader what is demanded gets published; what is not wanted, be it never so valuable, soon ceases to be produced. From every indication it seems that criticism does not belong to the latter class, and has not for over two centuries. Moreover it is increasing in quantity and quality to meet corresponding demands. Even volumes of Essays in Criticism, gathered perhaps from Reviews where they were published months or years apart, and strung together on the slenderest thread of concord—such volumes are bought and read with eagerness, provided the author is an authority in the domain of criticism. These books are read as literature as well as books about literature. Thus they have a twofold interest and value, and their writers a double opportunity.

Some have seen this and have made the most of it. They have helped to build up a literature of criticism worthy to take its place beside the literature of history and philosophy, of the sciences and the arts, of poetry and fiction. They have redeemed it from mistakes and disgraces in the past and given it a new name and a new purpose. Therefore they have done it a praiseworthy service by securing for it an honourable place in the kingdom of letters, and for themselves the gratitude that is due to reformers of the old and inspirers of new methods and principles in criticism.

XVI

READERS AS CRITICS

"He must be a wise man who knows what is wise."
                                        XENOPHON.

ALL criticism of books, as of life, is not printed.   Perhaps it is well that it is not. Spedding, in his *Life of Sir Francis Bacon*, suggests that this would be a better world if everyone should tell his neighbour just what he thought of him! Possibly this might be the case after the first century of friction was over, and all men had become accustomed to unrestrained and unlimited criticism; but who would wish to live in that century ? It is a proposition to be speculated about rather than to be carried into immediate practice.   The records of one association of young men who made the experiment hardly warrant its universal adoption.   Yet, in a measure, such criticism of life and letters is going on continually, and in so large a degree

256

that, of all a community who are passing judgment, the only person who is not taken into its confidence, and who does not join in its strictures, is the person or the author who is criticised. He may see what gets into print, but he knows only a thousandth part of what judgments are passed upon his work by its readers.

A numerical calculation will make this clearer. Suppose that a thousand copies are issued of a new story by an author unknown to fame. A hundred may go to reviewers who will give their opinion of it in a hundred paragraphs. These judgments will be noted with care or indifference, as the case may be, and the impressions they convey be remembered or forgotten with the rest of the " general intelligence." Nine hundred other readers of the book will form an opinion of their own, modified possibly by the critics, but influenced more by their own impressions. These in turn will be a resultant of sensibility, prejudice, literary acumen, education, and other factors which enter into judgment. If some of these nine hundred reader-critics are too indifferent or incompetent or indolent to form an opinion, the relative proportion of thinking readers to the professional reviewers will be kept by other hundreds who read every volume in addition to the buyers of it. . This number

17

is also greatly increased by the readers who draw the volume from public libraries. By any computation the outspeaking critics outnumber ten to one the judges who submit their opinions in writing and in print. Augustine Birrell remarks with truth: " The pen may, in peaceful times, be mightier than the sword, but in this matter of criticism of our contemporaries the tongue is mightier than the pen."

As numerical tests are now being considered, it may be asked, How many other reading people does the verdict of one intelligent reader reach ? This is not so easy to compute owing to differences in social surroundings, communicative habits, and personal recognition. Each one who is not a recluse has his own group composed of those who gather about his table, meet him in business, in clubs, and in society. In some of these places talk will run upon books, and the sentiment of the thinking man will go for something. Not so much personally as in Doctor Johnson's day of autocracy in literary judgment, but still for something. In these days the chief power and value of individual estimate is in eliciting other personal opinions and thus establishing a consensus of a few to which the stronger minds furnish the principal tone and colour. In any case outspoken criticism reaches a few, and these few communicate the sense of it to others. Like the spreading of any report, especially if it be evil, no one can tell how many centres it is radiating from in a day after it has been started. The relative unimportance of comment about books as compared with that about persons is all that saves oral criticism from being as widespread as gossip.

Another question which naturally follows is, Of what value is the judgment of the reader-critic as compared with that of the writer-critic ? If it were left with the latter to answer, his thought might run to some clear-headed man *Relative value of readers' criticism.* of business or of leisure who has no inclination or temptation to print his opinions, but who has them nevertheless, and possesses qualifications and means of forming them, such as a large acquaintance with men and books, a sound judgment, few prejudices, and special knowledge in some department of learning. If deliberation characterises his thought and speech, all the greater will be the value of his estimates. Whatever they are they will have weight with those who hear them. They will be quoted with the added force of his name, until the outer circle is reached and they begin to appear original with the repeater of them,

or fall into the common stock of public opinion
whose contributors cannot all be identified.
The value of such opinion is measured by the
worth of the man who delivers it.   How great
this may be is seen when it can be decoyed
into print over the signature of a universally
recognised authority.   The multitude say, The
prince has spoken, and that is the end of it.
When the King of Omnoptera sneezes it is
binding upon the court to do likewise, and upon
the army to imitate the court, and the people
the army, until a grand sternutation has
sounded over the entire kingdom.   A few will
demur, for several reasons, but authority ultimately prevails according to its weight and its
reach.   There is also some deference to be paid
to the multitude of readers in what is called
professional life, students and specialists in this
and that who read widely, have opinions, and
express them in one way and another outside
the regular channels of criticism.   In this last
respect the writer-critic has the advantage of
such a reader-critic.   His constituency is limited
only by the thousands of people who are interested in book news; but perhaps the results
as measured by conviction and the aggregate
sentiment in a given community do not greatly
differ.   What one has heard Nestor say, above
all if he has discussed the matter with him, or

if he has heard it passed upon by a group of friends, is apt to become that person's conviction in its final form. A dozen reviews, especially if conflicting, would not unsettle it. He has filed it for future reference.

Then there is the great host of readers who do not wait for the opinion of any other person, but are satisfied with their own. They may not have the opportunity or the inclination to ask what another thinks. Their own impression is good enough for them; they are not anxious to have it disturbed. These doubtless outnumber all other critics. Their opinion may not be valuable but it is voluminous. Can the writer say that he cares nothing about it? Yes, just as he may say that he cares nothing about the speech of people. Nevertheless he does care. He would value it more than the dictum of the professional a hundred to one, if the latter would refrain from publication. It is cold type that he fears, and its power of making and circulating opinion. What is read is so much more formidable than what is spoken. Still the volume of oral criticism is powerful when it flows in a single direction, as it is apt to when fairly under way with the populace. It is something like the contagion of enthusiastic favour or malignant abuse which moves an excitable audience to applaud or condemn a speaker. Proximity and contact may be wanting, but the sentiment of a community or a nation is no contemptible force even if the holders of it cannot be gathered under one roof. When it is once in the air it may become as forceful as this same mild atmosphere is when moving at the rate of a hurricane.

Books have been published at rare intervals which illustrate the power of reader-criticism despite professional, as well as the fact that its favouring winds blow where they list and often unaccountably to critics. The most recent example is of a book[1] which has had all sorts of critical opinions passed upon it, but which, judging by its sales, has been in favour with some two hundred thousand purchasers during the last half year, and how many more who have taken pains to read it through each one can conjecture for himself. What is the cause ? The envious say, '' Judicious advertising.'' Perhaps so. If so, let it be tried upon the next novel that is published. The most effective advertising in this, as in some similar instances, has been the commendation of the book by those who have read it to those who have not, and by these in turn to others in an ever-widening circle.

Popular approval.

[1] Hall Caine's *Christian*.

The same influence of reader-criticism is observed in another work,[1] which our accomplished Ambassador at the Court of St. James pronounces " one of the most successful books of our time; written by a man who was not a writer, published by a man who was not a publisher, and read by people who never read." He adds very truly that " the wide reading of a book depends not so much upon how it is written as upon how much it is wanted." In this book it may also be said there are elements of truth and honesty, straightforwardness and simplicity, clothed with the modesty that generally goes with sterling worth — virtues all which the people recognise in his story as they did in the man and the soldier, the patriot and the chief magistrate. The value of the above graceful testimony is not diminished by the fact that the one who gives it was one of the authors of another biography which has been widely read, not because it was much advertised, but because a good life of Abraham Lincoln will always be in demand. The interest of the nation and other nations in two such men, and the recommendation of such books by every reader to his neighbour, are elements which are to be counted upon in the multiplication of editions more than the diver-

[1] *Memoirs of U. S. Grant.*

sities of criticism. Therefore Schopenhauer is wrong in his assertion that "the greater number of men do not form a judgment on their own responsibility, but merely take it upon authority; and that every man has just enough critical power to recognise those who are immediately over him." This may be true in Germany, but it is not here, where among other inalienable rights which the intelligent citizen exercises is that of literary judgment according to his abilities and his preference. These may differ in degree and character, but the composite result is a strong factor in the book-market.

This is often overlooked by the critics who have been accustomed to agree with Sheridan, that "the public do not undergo the fatigue of judging for themselves"; or with M. Caro, who accounts for the decline in public taste on the supposition that "each man reads by chance and judges by his own hasty and unreasoning impressions." Such sentiments are natural to the professional man when he contemplates those who "occupy the seats of the unlearned." If he will come down and sit among them he will find that if their opinion could be averaged, massed, and expressed it would be of sufficient power to be a "wind of

destiny " to many an author. There is sometimes, when the provocation is sufficient, a
silent ferment of opinion in the minds of the
public which has its own way of bursting forth
and upsetting the verdict of well-established
tribunals, making literature conscious not only
of printed strictures, but also of that criticism which is based upon the nature of the
general mind rather than upon personal impressions or professional codes. The popular voice
may not be divine, but it is effective by reason
of its very humanity. Lowell may have had
this in mind when he spoke of " a court of
final judicature whose decisions are guided by
immutable principles," and W. B. O. Pea-
body's half-jest contains a grain of truth when
he " consoles himself with the reflection, so
balmy always to courts of limited jurisdiction,
that the great appellate tribunal of the public
will remedy the evil by overthrowing our decisions." Instances where this has been done
will occur to students of literature, the verdict
of the critical jury being reversed by that of
what they might call the mob,—that public of
whom Du Maurier said, in matters of art, that
its judgment, though not infallible, is often
sound, " pleased they know not why, and care
not wherefore."

Another question is easier asked here than

answered, as to the degree in which this public sentiment influences professional critics, and thus indirectly finds expression in print. One solution might be found in that of the general problem in regard to the leading or following character of all journalism. Does it adopt oriental or occidental methods with the flock, and is the public led or driven; or like a stampeding herd does it sometimes drive the rounders-up ? No one can return an answer which shall be satisfactory to all, but there is reason to believe that the guardians and makers of public opinion keep a weather-eye upon its shifty movements. If the barometer is hung in the counting-room its indications are closely connected with the largest usefulness of the publication by increasing circulation, and not to watch it might be suicidal. Such heedlessness has proved the death of many journals, sometimes at the hands of a mob. Criticism, to be sure, is not so perilous as politics were before the Civil War, but neither is it insensible to atmospheric changes and influences. The critic, out of his den, is a man in the world open to impressions in conversation and from public opinion. He must be steel-armoured if the talk of the town does not filtrate through the layers of impersonality in which he wraps

Influence of popular judgment upon critical.

himself.   Or again, if he have a profound con-
tempt for the popular taste and judgment, the
common opinion of him may be reciprocal if
he should print his sentiments of scorn.

To some extent, then, it is fair to suppose
that the critic will be a spokesman for the
public when the book about which he speaks
has called forth a general expression of public
sentiment.   In so far he will serve the cause
of that greater criticism which is great by virtue
of its multitudinousness — that is, when it is
tolerably unanimous.   In the instance of a
powerful work it is apt to be so,—at least as
unanimous as the critics proper are.   Such
criticism by the multitude may not be termed
" the higher," but if numbers count in criticism as they do in government the critic cannot
afford to pass them by unheeded.

The question as to how far the general voice
is to be taken as a standard of criticism is one
which cannot be disposed of sum-
marily.   It is natural for the hun-   Public opin-
                                                ion as a
dredth man who can sum up and   standard of
                                               criticism.
distinguish the characteristics of a
writer to smile wisely over the ecstasies of the
ninety-nine who cannot tell why they are
pleased; but it is the pleasure that is of more
consequence than the analysis of its sources.
The wayside spring needs no chemist's certifi-

cate of its excellence, based upon his examination, however valuable this may be for a
municipal water supply or for peddlers of a substitute. The good wine needs no bush, and
the good book by some means is as sure to be
endorsed by the people as a good apple-tree to
be clubbed by urchins. Possibly it is safe to
say that the liking of the multitude of general
readers and the final judgment of the best
criticism are not far apart in regard to the essentials of excellence. The syntax of Bunyan
and the double meaning of De Foe, if he really
intended one, might be offences to the modern
critic, but as allegory or fiction there is little difference in the estimate of Christian and Crusoe
by the critical and by the uncritical. It would
require much destructive criticism to unsettle
general opinion about them. He who should
attempt it would fare worse even than the Ba-
conians in the Shakespeare controversy. And
so of all the people's books from Chaucer to
Longfellow. They may be works of genius or
of talent only, but they set the heart-strings
vibrating with their humour or pathos, and
compel assent to the truths they tell because
these are so true to our common nature. Such
books survive the time and fashion in which
they were written, and their trivial or glaring
errors are passed over for the greater virtues

they possess, as the spelling of Washington's writings was overlooked in the value of their counsels. In this matter of orthographic variation, it should be remarked, by the way, that the Father of his Country followed several royal precedents, as may be observed in sundry documents in the British Museum.

The chief difficulty in the question of popular standards of value is the length of time occupied in determining and fixing them. The book which the people are wild over this year may be forgotten in five years, or again they may be unmindful of one whose value will be discovered later. Owing, however, to the present attainments of criticism, the early experience of Shakespeare and Milton is not more likely to be repeated than that they will have successors in our time. It is far more probable that the promise of some work of fiction—or less probable that some poem—will create a popular furor of which the more sober-minded will be half ashamed a few years afterward, and wonder how they could have been swept into such intellectual jingoism. But if the popular sentiment of favour has, after divers risings and fallings, settled itself at a normal high-water mark, and has continued to maintain that position, a standard has been established which no critic can afford to disregard. Meantime he has the advantage over a public slow moving by reason of training and equipment, and can assist them in coming to a right judgment if they are disposed to be guided by him. Still their personal impressions will be as stubborn a factor to deal with as the critic's own, and if they are massed against his he must wait for that verdict of time which may confirm or reverse the decision of either party. The world, as well as the critic, outgrows its favourites, but both sometimes turn back with a lingering fondness to early ideals and the memories of childhood. Possibly this may explain much of the liking, more or less genuine, which the educated have for ancient classics. Unattractive as they were to youth, they were mixed up with the sports of school, and both are remembered together. Besides, the average reader does not dare run amuck of the accepted judgment of all time. He would deem himself a crank if he should proclaim his failure to appreciate Homer, Shakespeare, and the rest of the nobles. The general demand for their writings would also prove the correctness of his self-condemnation. Yet it has taken ages to establish their eminence before all the reading world.

It must be concluded, therefore, that in

criticism, as in other directions, permanent
values are the growth of time and the result of
many contributions and fluctuations of opinion.
The ordinary reader will have his own impressions, which may be modified by his neighbour's, and especially by authorities in criticism; but his own share in critical standards
will be like his vote in civil affairs and his
citizenship in the state, infinitesimal and belonging to the future in its best results. So is
a particle of earth, going with the current,
arrested by some object in the stream, and
countless other particles with it, until the accumulation in a bar turns the river into another
channel, and the bar itself becomes a bed of
clay, and finally a slaty rock, abiding as a landmark forever.

XVII

QUALIFICATIONS OF THE CRITIC

" It is a long or even a difficult piece of work to study a book: it is a delicate and complex operation to criticise it."— M. CARO.

SOME of the elements which enter into the composition of a critical mind have of necessity been intimated in speaking of what constitutes the best criticism. Beyond these there are qualifications which are personal as well as professional, differing with different persons in the same profession. If they were the same in all members of it, the profession itself would become stereotyped in its narrow, hard-and-fast methods, which might be worse than the free and unlicensed manner which now characterises it in certain instances. Still, as there are qualities which are always found in great military commanders and in leaders of men, in successful financiers, and in eminent judges, however much they may differ from one another

in personal appearance, modes of living, and
ways of thinking, so there are qualities which
distinguished critics possess in common, whatever their individual proclivities and tastes
may be.

First among these qualifications in their necessity to the judge of literary wares is Insight.
This is a comprehensive term. It
stands for more than discovery, dis-   *Insight.*
cernment, and perception, which it also includes.   It is to ordinary vision of things what
the penetrating, pervading power of the cathode
ray is to lamplight, daylight, and sunlight.
It is the mind's searchlight, finding the inner
reality hidden below the outer appearance and
clothing of thought, and especially its disguises
and misrepresentations.   Like its ancient con-
gener, Inwit, inner knowledge, it deals with
the innermost; is the inner sight which pre-
cedes the inner sense or accompanies it.   This
faculty serves different people in different ways
according to their need, but in general by furnishing each one with just the knowledge he
most needs.   To the business man it furnishes
the knowledge of the times and trade; to the
miner, of ore beds; to the mariner, of weather-
signs and sea-currents; to the politician, of
combinations for a purpose; to the ruler, of
the character of the men he is to trust in high

18

places. To the critic, insight is a clear perception of literary values in any writing. In order to perceive these values he must have the literary sense or faculty as a natural gift at first, and to be eminent in this vocation he must add to native power the strength that comes by discipline and use.

The line of its employment will not diverge far from that of creative composition. The critic will begin with the thoughts of the author as related to the chosen theme. Are they new enough or unfamiliar enough to be regarded as additions to the sum of what has been written previously ? To answer this single question implies a wide acquaintance with literature. In certain departments, especially in those of a semi-scientific character, it is easier to determine this than in those which have a continuous history, as philosophy for example. He must be well versed in the speculations of mankind in all time who can say whether or not a given proposition has been formulated heretofore ; and he will have a good memory if he can assign the time and place of its first publication and enumerate the occasions of its repetition. He will have unusual confidence in his erudition if he dares to say of any theory, This is a new discovery in the domain of truth. It may be new to him, but there are thousands of readers exploring the literature of every subject, with good memories of what they have read, and with good courage to challenge the announcement of a fresh discovery. The only safe assertion that most critics can make is : This thought, proposition, or theorem is unfamiliar to me, and so far as I am concerned it has to me the complexion of originality. So it may also have had to the author of it in this form. Every writer upon mental science may be supposed to know all that has been promulgated before his time; but this is taking much for granted. If he does not, and repeats what has been said before, the restatement may be new to him. Here will be an excellent opportunity for a critic to show both his knowledge and acumen — his knowledge in pointing to the place or places where the statement has been made previously; his acumen, in determining the probability that the author's knowledge equals his own. Or again, if there is at the close of the nineteenth century no originality except in the combination and re-combination of old truths, there will be a chance for the critic with insight to show how the author has improved, or otherwise, upon all former combinations, and has been felicitous, or otherwise, in adapting the latest to the needs of his own age.   For the statement which Aristotle or Thomas Aquinas or Bacon made will have been so different from what is needed now, that the restatement of an old truth may have something of the value of an original thought. The clear-headed critic will determine how much.   He will need both knowledge and insight to do this.

In some kinds of literature this determination of thought-values is of primary importance; particularly in the weightier departments whose business is with ideas rather than their expression, where writers are in pursuit of fundamental

Knowledge in the main departments of thought.

facts and principles.   Such books should go to specialists in their several domains; but specialists also are critics and have need sometimes of the graces of criticism.   Whereas, from the infrequency of their incursions into the halls of judgment, they are often more severe in their verdicts than those who habitually sit in the seat of the scornful.   In all kinds of books the thought in its relation to kindred thoughts and classes of thought is of supreme consequence. Therefore the judge of literature should make himself familiar with the chief provinces of truth as early as possible.   They are well defined, their outlines and main features can be ascertained without superhuman effort in these

days of digests, abstracts, and compends.
Enough can be learned to appreciate the erudition which has been gained by patient investigation. The more the critic himself has learned,
the greater will be his respect for those who
know more than he can ever hope to acquire in
a particular department, unless he abandons
the reviewing of general literature and devotes
himself to a specialty.

After the estimate of thought-values will
follow that of expression. It is here that
another phase of intellectual activity
comes in play. Insight is not so
much demanded as discernment,—
the power to discriminate between
what is fitting and what is alien to the thought
in the method and means of conveying it.
Discrimination, guided by right judgment, is
then the second qualification of the literary
censor. This faculty will be employed mainly
in the direction of diction and style, as insight
is in that of invention or finding of material.
Here perhaps is the place where the literary accomplishments of the critic are most apparent,
and the lack of them is chiefly to be deplored.
The criticism of diction is best attempted by
one who has at least a fair command of language himself. He will certainly need to know
the meaning of words and the force of syno-

nyms. His vocabulary will not of necessity be as large and varied as his author's; for many can see the beauty and fitness of phrases which they themselves could not have coined. But he should be able to appreciate the significance of a telling word, and the exact worth of it in the place where it is used. He will know if it is in place or out of place; if it is not appropriate here, although it might be elsewhere, and the reverse. Above all he should know the effective use of the common word, as Daniel Webster used common words, by emphatic placing and skilful combination, with the added advantage of ready apprehension. Besides the transparency and force which are apparent to every reader, there are subtle qualities which should be discovered by the critic, if they exist at all. The diaphanous simplicity of Matthew Arnold's essays, or of Arthur Clough's version of *Plutarch's Lives*, is perhaps the first excellence that prose should possess; but as there are many styles of architecture, so there are many orders of nobility in composition. A city of Hellenic temples would tire the traveller, and a library of books in the Attic manner would weary the reader. Accordingly the broad-minded judge will not let even an Asiatic wealth of decoration go unremarked and uncommended, if it be judiciously managed.   In poetry he will expect this, and in prose like Mr. Ruskin's he will discern the imaginative element as the natural outcome of a poetic mind dealing with themes which it could not well handle in verse, especially in its controversial moods.   Appreciation of tropes will depend somewhat upon the critic's own imaginative powers; but he should not undertake the first steps in literary judgment without a large endowment in the direction of the comparative faculty.

For it is in this sphere that one of the greatest possibilities for high achievement or disastrous bungling lies.   The imagination is a centrifugal force, continually flying off the orbit and path of straightforward understanding.   Its flights may have the graceful rise and return to earth of a projectile, or the uncertain soar of a balloon to vanish in clouds, get tangled in tree-tops, or lost in the wilderness. Its mission in composition is that of a side-light, illuminating what might otherwise be obscure.   Its rays therefore ought to be direct, not mystifying by cross-lights, nor distorting and bending like refractions in water.   To the fitting employment of the imagination, then, the critic may become a salutary guide, checking its erratic flights and commending its beneficent use.

There are other qualities of expression, greater and less, of which the verbal critic will take note, but his larger judgment will deal with such broader features of expression. as movement and proportion and unity, with grouping, adaptation, and emphasis.　These will be to his observation what the large phases of historic development are to the philosophic historical student as compared with the daily occurrences of the diarist. There is a satisfaction in tracing them which cannot belong to the petty events of the day and the month.　So the critic will enjoy the wider outlook toward the main features of the entire work which he is examining much more than in contemplating the wayside attractions or distractions that may be scattered here and there, however alluring or disturbing they may be.　Suppose, for example, that he is observing the movement of the discourse, be it oration, narration, or novel.　He will look for conformity to the law of all movement in its tendency to increasing rapidity and force.　The laws of attraction and gravitation are not more inexorable in the material world than that of cumulative movement in the domain of consecutive composition.　This growth of the subject in interest and power should be expected by the critic.　When he finds it, it will be worth remarking, not because it is unusual, but because it is one of the large and indispensable features of discourse without which there will have been some sort of failure on the author's part.   His interest may have flagged, his stock of material run low through lack of diligence in collecting, or his industry may have slackened.   Any one of these causes or some other may be sufficient to check the momentum which otherwise is acquired in the natural expression of growing thought and the increasing sense of its importance.   If so checked, the impression is conveyed of waning interest and power, of incompleteness and partial failure.   The book that does not carry its reader with sustained attention to the end becomes for that reason obnoxious to just censure, for it has not fulfilled the first condition of living thought, which is growth.

Another condition will be an object of the critic's legitimate inquiry, and that is proportion.   After growth, or with it, should be found symmetry.   The ease with which this is violated is as apparent in a composition as in a tree which is growing one-sided, too low, or too high.   There are few perfect trees, to be sure, owing to interferences by other trees, to untimely accidents, early twists and bendings and bitings, to violent winds and repressing shadows, to lack of good soil and plenty of room and nourishment. Similar causes dwarf and warp works of literature whose growth is vigorous enough, but whose development is not preëminently symmetrical. The logic of them or the rhetoric is overdone; the narration and description crowd the dialogue; the episode is too long for the main thread of the story; the plot is too feeble or too intricate. There is overloading somewhere, and the movement is irregular in consequence. Where these irregularities and protuberances and deficiencies are, the critic will point out; but in doing so he will also find his judgment taxed to take extensive views and to make comprehensive estimates. It is much easier to analyse passages instead. Mr. Lowell has indicated this in a remark upon the prevailing style of criticism which dwells upon parts of a composition rather than the whole, the beauty of single paragraphs instead of the general symmetry. "These," he adds, "are good when they lead to something, like passageways, but not to dwell in."

Only a superficial study of literature is requisite to convince one that real excellence depends rather on the sum of a writer's powers than on any brilliancy of special parts. This the critic will keep in mind, and remember that

what an author will be valued for the longest
is the average of his work. This will include
his highest achievements here and there ; but
not upon these alone will his enduring fame
depend. The general proportion and due distribution of discussion and illustration, of reason and fancy, of sobriety and lightness, of fact
and figure, each in its place, will be what the
sound judgment will look for and approve.

It is such proportionate treatment that contributes to still another excellence which may
be called Unity. This is chiefly the relation of
every part to the central proposition, out of
which discourse grows as the tree from an
acorn. Back to this root principle the critic
will try to trace any paragraph and any line in
an entire book. It may be as remote from the
trunk proposition as the outermost leaf is from
the stock of a tree, but the line of connection
should be as direct as the channels through
which the sap rises and recedes from the nether-
most root to the topmost twig. There will be
nothing to interrupt or sever this clear connection. If there is, it is the business of the critic
to show where and how this is done, and if the
paragraph or sentence belong to some other
topic than this which the author is unfolding.
So will he be serving the interests of unity in
composition, and incidentally teaching con-

formity to the law of unity which prevails throughout the entire world of matter and mind. It is this which satisfies the craving for oneness, and delights the thinking man, and the unthinking also when he least suspects the cause. The whole mental predilection is towards the manifestations of unity and away from division and disintegration. Therefore the paragraph, the chapter, and the book should conform to this principle. If they do not they will be open to just criticism: for whatever any literary composition may lack of strength or beauty or grace it must not be wanting in unity. If it is, there will result in effect two or more productions instead of one.

The larger the work is, the more difficult, of course, it becomes to maintain and to discover its oneness. Different parts clearly indicated and distinct chapters in each part aid both the writer and the reader to distinguish the main and subordinate divisions. But like the larger and lesser branches of a tree they should be readily traceable to the parent stock, the single-germ idea.

In addition to the larger features of movement, proportion, and unity there is the question of the author's method of accomplishing his purpose. Is it in accord with the tenor of that purpose, and is it the most effective he might have employed ? The answer depends largely upon the object he has in view. If it is one which addresses the under-standing, the critic will look for plain and clear exposition. Statements will be direct and well substanti-ated. Processes of reasoning, if argumentation be necessary, will be as simple as is consistent with flawless logic. Here the critic himself will need special furnishing in a direction where it is possible to deceive one's self and be en-trapped by another. In a case where he may be sure that something is wrong it may be difficult to determine where the fallacy lies, whether in a false premise or an unsound con-clusion. Yet something more may be required by the reader than an assertion that the reason-ing of the author is poor. This is always the supposition when he does not happen to agree with the reader. He is sophistical or illogical or betrayed into inconsistencies by his own prejudices. It is the business of the one who sits in judgment to be able to show just where the weak link is which determines the strength of the chain; or again it may be equally obli-gatory upon him to prove that the reasoning process is sound from beginning to end. Not many critics will wish to stop to do this,—a guess or a personal opinion is easier; but it is such painstaking that makes the difference between one judge and another, and establishes the character and reputation of one over another. Other things may be decided by taste, but ratiocination is as inexorable as mathematics in its criteria, and the truth or falsity of logical processes is as capable of demonstration as a problem in geometry by those who know how to apply unfailing tests.

Some logical training will, therefore, constitute a part of that man's critical furnishing who is able to sit in judgment upon such a work, for example, as Drummond's *Natural Law in the Spiritual World*, or Argyle's *Reign of Law*, or Darwin's *Descent of Man*. These, to be sure, are in the upper ranges of literature and science and of human thought; but as it is easier to follow than to lead, to understand than to discover and reveal, so the able reviewer ought to appreciate the road-breaking service that has been done, and be enough of a pioneer himself to follow close in the path which the author has blazed and to show its bearing to the army of readers. He will indicate, first, if the subject is best treated by exposition and argumentation, and then say whether the statements are clear and the reasoning sound.

So likewise if the author has chosen to convey his message by narration and description, by dialogue and monologue, there is usually abundant opportunity to determine whether these are the best media, and if they have been employed to the best advantage.   Into this class of writing *Criticism of historical writing.* enter all the books of a descriptive character, whether of events and men or places and times. Historical statements of what has occurred in any past period belong preëminently to such composition, and nothing is more liable to criticism than historical writings.   The difficulty of obtaining trustworthy material in the conflict of contemporary statements, the uncertainty of tradition, the diversity of early records in their testimony, all furnish chances for exceptions to be taken by the accomplished judge of historical literature.   Add to this the theories, or possibly the prejudices, of the historian himself, and still further advantage is given an impartial judge to demur to conclusions, if not to original statements.   But his own qualifications must be commensurate with the undertaking in hand if he will justify his attempt to readjust statements with which he does not agree.   For this reason such judgment is seldom undertaken except by experts, who sometimes have a position of their own to maintain and a theory to defend.   It is too large a field for the novice or the uninformed to enter, if they have their own credit at stake or that of their publication. Nevertheless, that class of critics " who rush in where angels fear to tread " is not extinct. Possibly being at home in some corner of the house historic, in closet, cellar, or garret, they are ready to dispute with the author about the entire edifice, its past owners and the lives they lived, its builders and the way they builded. It is of no avail to mention the cobbler whose critical ambition tempted him beyond his last, nor to remind them of the rebuff he got. The little knowledge which is proverbially so dangerous is chiefly so to those who stand in front of it. The recoil seems to be feared no more by the 'prentice hand in criticism than that of a pistol by an urchin. Yet a pellet of small calibre can do a disproportionate amount of damage to a piece of statuary, though seldom injuring the sculptor. Even the critical sunshade of a woman, pointing out with too much emphasis a defect in Apollo's marble harp-string caused the fragile cord to snap, and incidentally payment to be made for the broken lyre—and the statue also. Occasionally, too, aggressive judgment strikes backward as well as forward. This used to be the case in the days when criticism was frequently personal vituperation, and the abused party sought redress in the

courts, and often obtained compensation.
Even when mild but incorrect strictures have
been made, heavy damages have in some instances been awarded.   Hence the advantage of knowing something about the laws of
libel.

However perilous it may be to make qualifying remarks upon the more solid forms of
literature, such as works of history   Criticism of
and biography and scientific treatises   fiction.
of any kind, there is one department of letters
which is regarded as an open field of exercise for
all comers.   Everybody can read fiction, and
by reason of its peculiar and personal interest
almost everyone can formulate his impressions and pronounce his judgments.   Moreover there is so much novel-reading that the
army of amateur critics is a vast one.   It is
largely made up of volunteers, to be sure,
but out of such an host excellent material is
sometimes developed for the regular service.
Indeed it might be discovered upon investigation that our best critics of fiction have come
up from the ranks of unprofessional readers.
Their aptitude was not known even to themselves until they began half unconsciously to
betray the gift that was in them.   Encouraged
by friends or circumstances they went on from
one venture to another until recognition in the

high places of journalism and literature crowned them with approval.   Still there are all degrees of attainment scattered along this road to eminence.   Probably, too, there would be no superlative achievement if there were not considerable struggling, indifferent performance, on the upward path.   Therefore for the ultimate gain much commonplace endeavour should be encouraged when it is nothing worse than commonplace.   Out of much strenuous labour on the part of the aspirant, and some annoyance on the part of authors, good may come at last to the literature of romance through estimates of it more or less judicial made by those who have not yet attained pre-eminence.   Such may welcome the suggestion of a few particulars in which their labour may be judiciously expended.

It will be remembered first and often that the work of fiction should be, for the reader's purposes, a true representation of life and character, individual or collective.   It differs from history and biography in not being a literal transcript of some particular experience or character.   But it is expected to be the reflection of possible characters and events in the romance, and of probable, every-day circumstances and personages in the novel.   In accordance with these two types of fiction, judgment will be passed upon their limitation to their respective bounds. The romance may no doubt deal with the ordinary affairs of life and with commonplace characters upon occasion, but it must not be surprising if the critic avails himself of his privilege to insist that the story shall throw a glamour of strangeness over all events and characters, seeing that the author is writing a romance rather than a novel. The critic, on the other hand, will not demur if the romancer run clear up to the borders of the impossible, provided he do not cross over them into the dim realms of the incomprehensible: for there is a region beyond that which is possible according to natural laws, which may be imagined by an extension of their working, which is not comprehensible within their natural modes of operation. Such ventures into the domain of the preternatural as the excursions of Poe and of Jules Verne will be estimated upon their own lines and by a special code.

Of the ordinary romance the critical reader will demand only that it keep within the limits of that possible world which is supposed to be more interesting than the one we inhabit. In this sphere To the bounds of possibility. of romance, however, such laws as those of gravity and sound and light and sensation will

operate in the customary way. The reader
will be justified, for instance, in demanding
that the hero shall not escape from peril by
remaining under water as a whale might, or
that he shall not be transported through the
air in anything less substantial than a balloon,
or that at last he shall not be shot with a noise-
less gun, although smokeless powder may now
be permitted. There may likewise be a question as to the amount of glamour that can
legitimately be cast over an ordinary experience, such as the entrance into a house in the
daytime and when the family is at home, or
the act of eating,—drinking may have illusions
of its own corresponding to the quality and
quantity of what is imbibed. There are also
limits to the grandeur and the stateliness, the
weirdness and the unnaturalness of every-day
life, even in kings' courts and queens' apart-
ments. Those who are best acquainted with
the ways of various orders of nobility will say,
that most of the distinctive features which
separate their mode of living from that of
persons equalling them in resources exist largely
in the earldoms and dukedoms of the imagination. Royalty itself has its cozy retreats from
the vastness and discomfort of castle halls and
stately rooms of ceremony, which are inhabited
by princes in story alone.

On the other hand, if the author in any manner advertises the romantic nature of his volume, he will be subject to mild censure if he does not deal in mysteries, surprises, and adventures out of the common.   They are not all to be so strange as the rare occurrences which are stranger than fiction, because there is no verisimilitude to romantic life in a succession of shocking catastrophes or of ecstatic experiences.   With the introduction of a larger proportion of these terrors and raptures no fair-minded judge will quarrel.   The shock and the thrill are expected, and the reader is naturally disappointed in an electric age if he does not receive electric treatment.   For that matter, our predecessors were even more exacting than ourselves. Heroes raved and heroines wept to produce a sympathetic and imitative action on the part of readers, while critics pronounced that romance a failure which did not draw sighs from their own hearts of steel, and tears from their judicial eyes.   Sometimes they chose to storm and bluster in order to hide their weakness, or let tears of laughter stand over to cover signs of alternating sympathy; but in any case it was the sensational that they demanded for themselves, and by consequence for their followers, the reading public.

The uncommon and marvellous.

When the modern novel is to be estimated, other qualities will be exacted by the judgment of the best readers. This type of *The novel of realism in its best sense.* literature in these days makes the claim of simply " holding the mirror up to nature," and as nature is supposed to be very commonplace in its daily moods, fidelity in reflection is all that is to be expected. Out of this general principle realism and naturalism in their various phases have been evolved. The better sort deal with the life and characters of such people as may be met on every corner, in situations such as occur somewhere every day in the week. The inquiry that the critic will make will be with respect to the faithfulness of the portraiture to existing types of men, women, and children, together with the correspondence of incidents to those which are taking place day by day. Particularly he will ask if the author has drifted too near the violent display of emotions which belong to romance, and the coarser conduct that proceeds from anger, hatred, revenge, and passions of similar strength, bad or good. Instead of these he will look for delicate portrayal of the finer phases of character, employing themselves in ways corresponding to the *finesse* of modern life and manners, as effective as the brag and bluster of the olden time.

Then there is the novel which attempts to interpret some tendency of the time, such as the widening of the chasm between the rich and the poor, the fashionable and the unfashionable; or the centralisation of wealth and the dissemination of letters and learning, intelligence and culture. Even methods of religious manifestation and of social development are not now beyond treatment by the writer of fiction, to whom no combination of present forces is impossible, nor any wild conceit which can be imagined in the progress of future ages.   To keep these imaginings within the bounds of reasonable probability and possibility and of logical succession, and to keep both the millennium and ultimate chaos at their normal distance, is a part of the critic's useful mission.   He at least is to keep his own head level amidst the general pirouetting and cavorting of speculative and spectacular novelists.   Also he is to be in sympathy with any effort that is honestly made toward improvement in popular wisdom, socially, politically, or religiously.

When he comes to the novel of the reformer, however, he will need a clear sense of what reform is, and of the actual evil to be reformed. There can be no denial of the good work done by the school of writers of which Charles Reade was the pioneer, and Charles Dickens the most eminent example. The treatment of criminals in prison and in penal settlements, of patients in lunatic asylums, and of children in schools, of young and old in manufactories, and similar class and caste oppression, has furnished the motive of much powerful fiction, which in turn has helped to sweep such wrongs from civilised communities. When books with such a good purpose appear, it is the critic's opportunity to show his sympathy with their object, even if the manner of accomplishing it should be subject to strictures, so far as the literary performance is concerned. Dickens himself, with more or less justice, has been called a caricaturist, and his method of portrayal sentimental. At other times he has been designated as a satirist, romancist, or fanciful humourist, devising unskilful plots and improbable incidents; but some of the critics who have objected to the motive of his novels with a purpose have been those who possibly were in practical sympathy with the social evils which he attacked without fear or favour. They afford striking instances of the bias which interest can give to judgment. It is such novels as these that give the reader a chance to discriminate in his verdict between the author's purpose and his execution, his attempt to right a wrong and his failure, or success perhaps, in choosing the best vantage-ground for the battle, and in conducting the fight in the most effective way.   At all events the critic will not allow his censure of manner to extend to condemnation of purpose. He loses his judicial reputation if he does, and shows his fairmindedness if he does not; a great loss in one instance, and a great gain in the other.

In this connection it may be remarked that the older reviews and critics did yeoman service in Great Britain for reforms of various kinds.   The *Edinburgh Review* especially

"urged the repeal of the game laws, the improvement of prisons, the protection of chimney-sweeps and other social unfortunates.   It attacked pedantry and tradition, ridiculed the narrowness of university ideals, and argued for toleration in religion. Living topics, political and social, were discussed in the light of the very latest ideas."

Such reform-criticism marked the opening of the nineteenth century.   It was not asked so much, What new books have appeared ? as What topics just now are best worth discussing? With a book-title for a heading an independent discussion of the same subject would often follow.   The book itself might not be referred to again. This, however, while it might be creative literature, was not critical in the strictest sense.

The day of that sort of reviewing has passed. The critic of the present time usually sticks to the book he has in hand, or sometimes to a group of them on the same topic, noticing the bearing of each on the general subject. Very rarely now is a book made the occasion for the reviewer to enter upon a ventilation of generalities upon its theme in order to fill space and avoid saying much about the author's treatment of it. The reasons for such procedure are best known to the reviewer, and may differ with different cases. He may have little to say, or may wish to say little. Or he may have too much to say for the space allowed him.

In enumerating a few of the qualifications belonging to a critic of general literature, some Recapitula- notice of different kinds of writing tion. has been needful; also so much specification of his attitude toward them as to make more particular suggestion unnecessary in this place. The main requisites will be remembered as insight and a wide knowledge in the main departments of human thought and interest, as well as of the cardinal principles and larger features of expression, and a sense of the author's methods in accomplishing his purpose, whether by narration of facts or portrayal in fiction. Beyond these general principles, and growing out of them, each critic will find minor principles, precepts, and maxims suited to his own taste, temperament, and judgment according to the law of liberty and to liberty under the laws.

XVIII

THE CRITIC'S RIGHTS

" Equity is according to the conscience of him that is chancellor."—SELDEN.

AUTHORS should remember that critics have a few rights reserved. Even the criminal at the bar can claim as much, the accuser more, and the judge more still. In whichever category the incensed or outraged writer places the cause of his woe, the offender will be found to possess " the inalienable rights of life, liberty, and the pursuit of happiness "—also of pursuing the author. The critic himself will be likely to emphasise the third and fourth of these privileges; the first and second being granted by fundamental law. The degree of professional liberty and the means of securing personal happiness in his profession are matters about which disputes will always occur between writers and critics of books. The latter will maintain that personal independence is the bulwark of efficiency and usefulness in literary judgment. The author will retort that it is too dangerous a prerogative to be accorded to any man unless he speak in the first person singular and sign his strictures or estimates or appreciations with his own name, avoiding the royal and editorial " we," and not borrowing the authority of the entire staff, if he belongs to one.

But the weight of custom is against this sentiment, and the balance of power is with the free-lance, as the journalistic army is at present constituted. When so much can be said on both sides with some show of reasonableness, it may be that the question of ethical rights may be one of qualification and modification. They are not to be totally denied the critic, nor should he insist upon unrestrained license to ravin like a wolf. His liberty, like all true liberty, ought to be under the regulation of laws. But what laws ? Some of them have been indicated already as rules deduced from the art of poetry and prose, of fiction and fact in literature. These, however, relate to the technique of his own art. What is now to be considered belongs rather to the general freedom of his pen.

This might be considered as a part of the larger subject of the freedom of the press, being intimately connected with it ; or, again, with the still more important topic of the freedom

License limited. of opinion to be expressed when and where and in what manner the individual thinker pleases. Undue license, running into libel, the laws take care of ; but there may be much harm done outside the limits set by the laws. It was in the hands of Hoder the blind, directed by Lok the accuser, that the fatal mistletoe, considered too insignificant to be included in the general oath of fealty, slew Balder the good. There are scurrilous sheets which have learned by familiarity with prosecution that there are forms of insinuation which present no retaining point for the law to seize upon. Damage can be done as effectually and much more safely by the ruminating question than by the dangerous assertion. All such cowardly methods are, of course, below the lowest grades of criticism, and to be brushed aside in clearing the way to the actual rights of the judge of literary performance.

If he is what the above term implies, he must be permitted to use his own judgment.

Right of personal judgment. He certainly will not depend upon another's. More than in any other department of intellectual labour he must preserve his own individuality and do his own thinking. In science some reference must

be had to other men's discoveries and conclusions; in art one will be somewhat influenced
by prevalent theories and practice; in creative
literature the fashions of the time will unconsciously affect the writer.   Although the same
may be true in the domain of criticism, there
is all the more necessity that the judge be
allowed a large independence in his thinking.
In the present indeterminate state of the science one's own impression will become the
foundation of his judgment, upon which he
will build according to principles of equity and
catholicity, understanding and sympathy.

It is in this as in matters of conduct.   The
individual conscience must be the guide and
director of each person.   '' Thine The literary
own and not another man's '' is a   conscience.
rule as old as the Pauline Epistles.   For the
rights of this conscience and its supreme
authority men and nations have been eloquent
in words and deeds and sufferings.   Now what
the conscience is to the man who is making his
way amidst the perplexities of daily life, the
literary sense is to the critic.   He must follow
its leading.   He would not be an independent
judge if he should ask another man what he
ought to think, and what verdict he ought to
pronounce, however valuable that other man's
impressions and opinions may be.   The indi-

vidual and independent opinion may be wrong and far out of the way, but it is the right one for the person himself because it is his own. His independence may cost him everything but the consciousness that he has lived up to his light and has done the best he could. If he fails continuously he will conclude that criticism is not his calling and try another.

But there is a further parallel to be drawn between the literary and ethical conscience. No one has a right to say that the latter is the best possible guide until every pains has been taken to inform and educate it. Examples are abundant of this disparity between acts and conduct before and after illumination. The same may be said of the literary conscience as of the moral. That there is such a thing as conscience in literature Mr. Arnold has clearly shown, and he has admirably defined it in the case of the French nation. He calls it

Should be an educated conscience.

" a deference to a higher standard than one's own habitual standard in intellectual matters ; a respectful recognition of a superior ideal caused by sensitiveness of intelligence. And those whose intelligence is quickest, openest, most sensitive, are readiest to pay this deference."

This recognition of a lofty ideal will compel

every critic to modify his independent views.
He may have the professional right to pronounce
judgment according to the dictates
of his personal literary conscience,   *Modifying personal opinions.*
but the same conscience will require
him to give it the best possible education. He
will not substitute independence for information, if he has a reputation for fairness to make
or maintain. If he attempts to pass judgment
on a work of fiction or of fact, he will need
something more than his likes and dislikes to
go by. He will ask if there is a superior tribunal which may reverse his decisions, and in
this way pronounce sentence upon him as he
has upon his author, but with a greater weight
of authority than his own. Theoretically every
critic is supposed to speak for himself in his
own time and way; but it is easy to imagine a
deferential waiting among the guild until some
chief has uttered his dogmatic pronouncement,
which lesser lights may safely follow with such
variations of phrase as may give an appearance
of independence and originality. It is so in
other departments of thought, opinion, and
doctrine. Can anyone safely say that the
domain of criticism is free from deferential following of leaders? It would be well if there
were even more of it than there is,—good at
least for literature; for then good work would

20

have somewhat of uniformity in its approval, and indifferent and poor performance would be rated at its value without exception. How to strike a balance between the independence of the individual critic and a due amenability to recognised authority in the republic of letters is still an unsettled problem. At present literary judgment is much like another kind that prevailed in the disordered time of Israel's judges: " In those days there was no king in the land, but every man did that which was right in his own eyes." It was the carnival of license and personal freedom of judgment. But the legitimate result was inconvenient to travellers, and they demanded a strong and recognised authority to mete out justice.

In this respect the Continent of Europe has for good or ill and from time to time attempted to establish the concurrent authority of several in the place of individual opinion. Imitating the ancient coteries of literary men as far back as Ptolemy Soter at Alexandria, and the liberal caliphs at a later day throughout the Mohammedan countries, the Medici's schools of philosophy became precursors of learned academies in every city. What six hundred of them did as a sort of judiciary in letters may be guessed from the name of the most enduring and influential of them all, " The Academy of Bran and Chaff," in allusion to its object of " purifying and winnowing the national tongue." Its dictionary is still considered as the standard authority for the Italian language after revisions for two hundred and eighty-five years; and, incorporated with two other societies, the academy continues an organisation that was begun over three centuries ago under the present name of the Royal Florentine Academy. France was only fifty years behind Italy when Cardinal Richelieu instituted the *Académie Français* in 1635, which, after various deaths and revivals, still preserves the original name, meeting twice a week to take care of the French language, to publish French classics, and in some of its branches to exercise authority as judge and censor of literature. Other nations of Europe, Great Britain excepted, caught the infection at an early date and established high courts of literary judicature. In spite of them all, however, perhaps on account of them all, eminent individual critics have arisen from time to time, some of them members of academies and some not, who would doubtless have said that they were a law unto themselves. Still, no man could live under the shadow of these academies and not be affected by their influence.

At the same time there has usually been

sufficient freedom under the laws of these literary republics to permit of a wide range of personal taste, opinion, and judgment. If there has been any constraint it has been that self-restraint which everyone exercises in the presence of the public sentiment of the best in any community, according to the prevailing ethical or literary standard of the age. Those who defer to prevailing standards will always be more truly free and more genuinely independent. Their rights will be more because of the respect granted them; their privileges greater by reason of their citizenship and the official standing accorded them as representatives of the best sentiment and soundest judgment of their contemporaries.

To one, therefore, who is inclined to insist upon the exercise of his private opinion at all hazards it should be recommended that he first conjecture whither it will lead him, and what its value will be in the market-place of opinions. If opposed to the best thought of his time, will it be worth parading and insisting upon? What will be its reflex action, and where will the possible recoil land him? Of course there is the "courage of convictions," about which there is always much martyr-like talk, which, moreover, is always to be maintained by honest men and brave. But what if these convictions should not be worth defending ? There has been much heroic suffering for mistakes and foolishness, as well as considerable exhibition of them with boldness. Accordingly the valorous critic might well write over his desk the inscription above three of the gates of Egyptian Busiris: " Be bold," " Be bold," " Be bold " ; and add with profit the legend over the fourth gate: " Be not too bold."

A question has been raised at times respecting the right of a critic to withhold his name from his work. It would seem that he should have the same privilege of *Anonymity.* anonymity that is accorded to any writer. If Sir Walter Scott chose to watch the public puzzling over the authorship of his novels, and to listen to the criticisms of the crowd as he mingled with it rather than to enjoy a more direct tribute of praise, no one could deny his right to do so. The same may be said of all imitators of his secrecy, even if the imitation extend no farther: also of all writers of worthy books about which the authors for one reason or another have chosen to throw the veil of mystery. It is their own affair, and is attended with a kind of self-denial. They are not receiving the best, and sometimes the only, reward of their labours.   Often a less modest claimant has carried off the honour for a time, compelling the author to come forth from his hiding-place and appropriate his own creation and the credit of it.   Others, like *Junius*, cannot be smoked out of their burrows by laudatory incense, nor entrapped by guesses of forty names not their own, nor decoyed to accept a brilliant literary fame with the qualifying inconveniences which a surrendered anonymity is apt to entail.

There are, however, better reasons than curiosity and mysteriousness why a critic should not always reveal his identity.   If he is to be the representative of impersonal justice in literary matters, he should remain impersonal to the public as far as possible.   The moment he is recognised, his judgments are associated with what is known or suspected about him.   His antecedents, his education, affiliations, religious beliefs, political alliances, and literary prejudices—some or all of these suffice to qualify and account for anything that he may say with which his readers do not agree.   By so much as they can in this way explain, is his critical judgment discounted.   It must be confessed that there is sometimes considerable ground for such qualifications to impartial judgment, but the critic, like other suspects, has a right to avail himself of all the advantages in his favour. Accordingly he may decline to declare his name so long as no damage is done to the life, property, or reputation of others. Their feelings, so called, are not to be taken into account. An author should have none, or at least should not expose them on the highways of literature to be held up by masked marksmen, or in the market-place to be fired at from behind closed shutters. For it is essential to the weeders-out of the indifferent and worthless that they be accorded the absolute freedom in their good work which anonymity alone can secure. Publicity would subject them to inconveniences,—perhaps not so great as in the horse-whip days of Berkeley and Fraser, or the duelling times of Moore and Jeffrey; but there are weapons more effective than whip or pistol in literary hands, and some *Epistle to Peter Pindar* or *Battle of the Bards* may be surer in its aim and more deadly in result. All this would be of more effect if the critic were known; therefore his identity should be kept concealed lest he suffer harm and the cause of literature suffer with him.

On the other hand, the good that a fairminded critic can do under the shield of an incognito might be lessened if his name were subscribed to his judgments. Much that is done well is qualified by familiarity with the doer. From Benjamin Franklin and his two friends to the last signed article of a review, to say nothing of instances before Franklin's day, the prophet's honour has been beyond his own household and country, and imagination has been greatly helped by ignorance. How perilous would it be for most reviewers to pronounce upon anonymous literature that might be produced any year by our best writers! What a scoring some famous authors would get if they should happen to write an indifferent book in an off-year, under the cover of " Rejected Addresses " or of " authorship unknown "! Indeed it might be well for any who are disposed to trade on their prestige to send out now and then a production without the trade-mark, to see what the intrinsic value of the fabric would be rated at without the firm-label. Silversmiths often produce wares on which they refuse to place their sterling stamp, lest their reputation for good work be damaged. But the seal and superscription of authorship is the most valuable element to some traders in literature, judging by the publications in which eminent writers appear, and by what they occasionally allow to be printed over their signatures. Possibly the compensation is greater than for better work. If so, the whole transaction must be charged to popular standards of taste.

All the same, however, unendorsed productions are dangerous stuff for critics to handle who are not perfectly sure of the infallibility of their literary judgments. The best of them may slip now and then, like the old sexton in a metropolitan church who was famous for reading men at sight, so that more than one curious stranger presented himself before the magnate of the pews to see how far up the aisle he would be rated and seated. But there was a new " Fall of the House of Usher "! One day he placed a major-general in citizen's dress in the second pew from the door! The sexton's demise at an early day was attributed to his chagrin at a mistake which he made worse by an unfortunate attempt to correct it. Critics might easily err in the same manner if some of our magnates in the army of writers should be unrecognised in their fatigue costume. Nevertheless the critic's judgment would not be amiss in many instances. The illusion which goes with a great name among the people would be temporarily dispelled if the distinguished author's identity should suddenly be revealed, but the wisdom of the critic would be justified in spite of a brilliant reputation.

On the whole, then, anonymity may be the best position for both the criticiser and the criticised. Within self-respecting limits the one can pronounce juster judgments, and the other get the benefit of more impartial estimates of his work. The prejudice and spleen that are more possible to the anonymous reviewer will be their own antidotes, as the gall of a serpent is said to be the remedy for its bite. After all, such secrecy is a limited condition, and ends with the publication which endorses a review by printing it. Therefore the critic should be allowed his personal opinion, and the expression of it, and also the private keeping of his own good name. Publishers will see to it that he does not fall into chronic inaptitude, and will permit now and then a vagary for the sake of variety and the sensation it makes. Meantime the author whom it strikes may get a more effective advertisement, and incidentally a wider sale for his book than if it had been condemned " with faint praise " by one who was compelled to sign his critique.

It ought to be said that opinion on this matter is by no means uniform. A *Diverse views regarding anonymity.* name is demanded by some as a gauge of value in criticism, as in the instance of the person who said that the opinion of John Mill on a philosophical treatise would be worth all the anonymous reviews of it put together. Another asks, '' If a critic's own views are to be his rule of judgment, should not the community have the benefit of his signature ?'' Still another urges, that '' we feel a keener interest in signed criticism than in unsigned, because of a definite personality, —a real man speaks and not some impersonal method.'' It is an anonymous critic who says that it has been proclaimed that '' a man who calls himself ' We ' naturally takes airs which the singular ' I ' would avoid ''; and another, who ventures so far as '' G. B.'' toward a signature, remarks:

'' The pronoun *we* used by critics has a most imposing and delusive sound . . . whereas the criticism is generally the crude and hasty production of an individual, scribbling to oblige a bookseller or to defray current expenses ; but such is the magic of types that his crude decisions become circulated far and wide, and give or destroy reputation.''

A living author-critic speaking of the criticism of the early part of the century says, that '' this savage condition still persists in the toleration of anonymous criticism, an abuse that ought to be as extinct as the torture of witnesses "; and again, that " current criticism is conditioned in evil because it is almost wholly anonymous." One " G. H. L. " regards anonymity as " the parent evil of criticism "; and after arraying the common arguments in its favour under five heads he proceeds to answer them at length.[1] There is no ambiguity about Schopenhauer's sentiments on this question of anonymity :

" that shield of all literary rascality, a cloak for covering the obscurity, incompetence, and insignificance of the critic. For a man to wrap himself up and draw his hat over his face, and then fall upon people—this is not the part of a gentleman ; it is the part of a scoundrel and a knave. An anonymous review has no more authority than an anonymous letter, and one should be received with the same mistrust as the other."[2]

Le Gallienne is a trifle more charitable in being disposed to regard a critic as still a gentleman though anonymous, as Coleridge was inclined to think that a critic might be a gentleman when he had dropped his pen. Enough has been cited to indicate that there is a wide disagreement on this subject both among authors and critics, and, as is usual in

[1] *Westminster Review*, vol. xxxviii., p. 237.
[2] *Art of Literature*.

such bitter controversy, to show that strong reasons may be adduced for both sides. As criticism improves, and comes to take its place with other forms of literature, it is likely that successful writers of it will always be willing to be known, and to stand by their work, and take their chances at the hands of the critics of criticism.

There are one or two minor rights to which eminent critics themselves have called attention, that should not be overlooked. The right to Leslie Stephen points out that   blunder.

" every critic has a sacred and inalienable right to blunder at times . . . and if all who have blundered are to be pronounced incompetent, we should have to condemn nearly everyone who has taken up the profession. Not only Dennis and Rymer, but Dryden, Pope, Addison, Johnson, Gray, Wordsworth, Byron, and even Coleridge, down to the last new critic in the latest and most fashionable journals, would have to be censured. Still there are blunders and blunders, and some not easy to forgive."

Then there is the right of silence for the timorous, the uncertain, and those who would be glad to do a friend a kindly The right of service if they could conscientiously. silence. A reviewer of twenty years' experience thinks this a very simple rule under such conditions, and adds: " The right of silence is the only one of the Rights of Man for which I have the slightest respect, or which I should feel disposed to fight for." [1] How far this refusal to criticise is possible in the routine of professional reviewing is best known by those who are employed in it. If Bekker could be silent in seven languages, it is probable that critics can find ways to follow his example in one, when it is desirable to say nothing. Yet, as Coleridge remarks, " silence does not always mean wisdom."

[1] *Blackwood*, 161, p. 23.

XIX

RESPONSIBILITIES OF THE CRITIC

"I confess that criticism is not what it ought to be, not what it might be. But am I a bad critic, sir?"—CHRISTOPHER NORTH.

IT is more natural to insist upon rights than to recognise responsibilities. When these become grave, however, they lend a certain importance which often makes their possession a serious thing. This in turn is likely to impress a reasonable man with the necessity of carefulness in the use of his gift or opportunity. If these be great his solicitude will be correspondingly extreme, provided he be right-minded as well as able. If he be otherwise minded, the harm he may do will be proportionately great.

There may be departments of literature in which a writer can work good or ill to readers with more immediate or intense effect, —as in the novel of realism or naturalism, so called; but there is none in which more effect can be produced in the way of general impression. Hundreds of readers derive their limited knowledge of books and authors from notices and " opinions of the press." To the question, " Have you read such and such a book ? " a frequent reply is, " No, but I have seen a notice of it in my newspaper, or a review of it in my magazine." Nor is this to a reader's discredit. He cannot read the hundred or thousand readable books that are published each year and attend to other business. A careful estimate places the number of books that can be read by the average reader in eight hours a day for a year as about two hundred and twenty octavo volumes. It is doubtful if he can read this number and preserve his sanity, for more minds are injured by too much than by too little, beginning with newspapers and ending with the 'ologies. Such knowledge of current literature therefore as intelligent people desire to have, or need to possess, must be by abridgment, condensation, and summaries. These it is the province of the reviewer to furnish. He is the middleman between the author and the great multitude of readers wanting this and that and waiting for the signal which notifies them of its appearance in the market. Sometimes the want is created and curiosity aroused as by a new invention exhibited in a shop window.

The critic's first business, then, is fair interpretation. This is not advertising. The title of a book and mention of the house publishing it does that. The reviewer will say how far the contents Responsibility toward publishers. fulfil the promise of the title, so that people may feel safe in buying. To do this skilfully without giving away the gist of a volume or hundreds of volumes in return for a year's subscription, is not within the capacity of every reviewer. There is an opportunity here to ask about one's responsibility toward owners of copyright who have placed a volume free of charge in his hands. " Mere mention " may be an equivalent for its value, and no doubt is, in papers of wide circulation; but between this and stating all that is worth knowing of the work in hand there is great room for the exercise of a critical conscience. It is a matter of pecuniary responsibility, as much as belongs to a salesman who can increase or diminish his employer's custom. The main difference that can be urged is that the publisher of the paper is the employer in the critic's instance rather than the publisher of the books. A fair review, or an unfair one, cannot by any means affect the subscription list of a paper, as it may the book publisher's receipts, and incidentally the author's share in them as a return for his labour. Accordingly the generous critic will ask if he has any obligations toward the publisher. Of course such conscientiousness will be contrasted by the experienced with certain other consider-ations that sometimes weigh with both review-ers and their principals, but ideal work is what is being considered just now. With few ex-ceptions it is not to be admitted that the weighty name of a great publishing house can unconsciously affect literary judgment. What such houses publish is apt to be good, and their *imprimatur* is in itself a commendation to all readers, and in a measure to all reviewers. Still it is to be remarked that this does not always save a publication from sharp comment, de- ·served or undeserved.

The critic's conscience being clear with re-gard to his obligations to the publisher as a *Obligations to authors.* manufacturer, he will bestow a pass-ing thought upon the author. Of course this personage has challenged the critic by entering the arena with a printed book. It is a gauntlet thrown down with the expectation that it will be picked up as the gage of battle. Sometimes it happens that the volume is as the red serape of the *conquistador* to an infuriated bull. This is the case when there have already been attacks and repulses, criticisms and replies after the manner of Gifford and Leigh Hunt in the days of Quixotic chivalry in criticism.   This fashion is obsolete except in the back country of letters.   The battle of bookmen is no longer with pens dipped in venom, and seldom is any retort made by the author upon his critic, such as Swinburne and Thackeray and Tennyson made upon their reviewers in *Blackwood* and the *Times*.   The familiar reply of the Laureate to Kit North will be recalled:

> " You did late review my lays,
>   Crusty Christopher ;
> You did mingle blame and praise,
>   Rusty Christopher.
> When I learnt from whom it came,
> I forgave you all the blame,
>   Musty Christopher ;
> I could *not* forgive the praise,
>   Fusty Christopher."

Thackeray cut up a penny-a-liner in *An Essay on Thunder and Small Beer*, in which he " bantered Jupiter on his style, on his hoighth of foine language entoirely," and on his oracular pomposity in general.   Let these two instances stand for a long list of retorts from persons as illustrious as Dryden and Pope and Byron, not to mention numerous lesser lights.

With the passing of the pen-and-ink duel

also passed the opportunity of the author to retrieve his losses at the reviewer's hands, or at least to avenge his injuries and redress his grievances. He is *hors de combat* from the start, and the quarrel is all on one side according to the modern code. In view of this condition of things it is probable that critics have modified their methods. They forbear to strike a man when he is down. When a book with an honest purpose has been laid before them for honest appraisal they do not always regard it as a football to be kicked about and fallen upon. It is oftener considered as the product of diligence at least, and a part of someone's personality, into which time and labour and pains have been put for something besides a percentage of the sales. Respect for the motive of the writer prepares the way for a favourable consideration of the extent to which he has fulfilled the promise contained in title and preface. If this has not been met, of course no consideration for the way in which the author will receive qualification of his work can be allowed to weigh with the critic. The author has tacitly agreed to accept just judgment when he allowed his manuscript to go into type. Still he has a right to expect that judgment shall be just. The comity of the one-sided duel requires this, when the attacking party alone carries weapons. To be sure the author himself may have fired a scattering fowling-piece, charged with bird-shot, at a community, or may have discharged a broadside upon society at large, and thus merited the aim of some sharpshooter in return; but this rifleman ought to remember that the author cannot turn upon him personally, even if he could penetrate the screen of his ambush. Then there is the Golden Rule, which may be a higher law than is admitted among the ethics of criticism, but the code of critics would not be impaired by its presence.   The truth of this will be apparent to the reviewer when he turns from critical composition to creative, and becomes an author. According to the fable, nothing so clears one's ideas of justice in respect to gored oxen as to have one's own ox gored. The difficulty in treating others as you would be treated is in the strain upon the imagination which is required in putting yourself in another's place. Therefore the charge, often repeated, that critics are usually retired authors is not an invidious one. For the sake of the criticised they ought to be writers before they are judges of composition in order to appreciate its difficulties. They will thus be qualified to understand the meaning of Chaucer's lines:

"The lyf so short, the craft so long to lerne,
  Thassay so harde, so sharpe the conquerynge."

Still the courageous author will expect, not mercy and favour so much as justice, and will be glad if he always gets that and nothing more. If the critic is careful to accord this, his second responsibility will be met.

What is his third and highest responsibility? To readers, if he is what he ought to be, a true Responsibili- interpreter of literature. As an ty to readers. usher and judge he has some duties, but as interpreter he has more. Books get introduced without his intervention, and they are judged by others as well as by himself; but interpretation belongs especially to the reviewer. By this, in this place, is meant primarily, the truthful rendering of a book's main ideas into compendious and intelligible form, respectful of the author's rights, as mentioned above. He states why this author should receive the honour of a perusal by the reading public, giving the points deserving commendation which are supposed to be unknown to most readers. Or, again, his office may be to advise them not to read the book. In either case he has the great responsibility of a guide to a large constituency in the domain of literature. It may be said that readers are their own guides, and read what they choose; but it is also true that more people are " personally conducted " than are willing to admit such guidance.   At least they often make side excursions at the instance of book notices.   Therefore the pen that is behind these should consider its responsibility for the direction in which it points.   It may be answered that there is not unlimited confidence in " opinions of the press " on the part of those who know most about the necessities of their composition; but the knowing ones are a small proportion of the multitude who read and catch their impressions from the book-column. The rustic who vowed that a certain statement was true because he read it in his newspaper, belonged to a vast fraternity of the credulous and the impressionable.   All that journalists claim for the influence of the press may not be granted, but the aggregate power of many pages and many papers is greater than is sometimes imagined or conceded.   The reader may not recall what the critic wrote, but an impression that it was favourable or unfavourable remains, or possibly the recollection that there was some commendation and some qualification.   Of the two the latter is apt to be remembered longer than the former.

As a guide, then, to people who buy books and who read them the reviewer will have in mind his possible influence for good or ill, and therefore his responsibility. In proportion as he estimates his influence will he feel his responsi-

bility. He may be mistaken as to the actual degree of both, but that does not affect his conscientious dis-charge of a supposed obligation. According to his sense of his own importance his intellec-tual and moral accountability will be gauged by himself. Others will judge him by the ap-proach he makes to the standard of general opinion, which sooner or later determines the status of every book. By and by it will be known by readers and by all for whom he makes estimates how far his critical sense can be trusted. Daniel coming to judgment on others will himself be judged according to the truth of his verdict, and the pertinency of the saying, '' With what judgment ye judge ye shall be judged.'' This may be high ethics for the reviewer, but the highest is the widest in its application. There is such a thing as righteousness in the old sense of rightwiseness, even in passing sentence on the efforts of a contemporary in letters; and by this rightness both author and critic must eventually stand or fall. No maxim is truer than that injustice done another is likely to return upon the doer; and the bucolic proverb concerning chickens coming home is as true in criticism as in any other application of it. Its aptness in this case is equalled only by its homeliness and universality.

A step farther in this direction opens the larger question of kinds of literature that the critic will commend, and with which he will thus identify himself. He will not be suspected of endorsing false science or charlatanism of any sort, nor any glaring untruth in an age which professes to be seeking the truth in all its departments. There are, however, other departments of thought whose expression is more distinctly literature than scientific treatises, and more widely read. The broad fields of fiction and poetry and even the essay are open to all comers. As a consequence all sorts of writers are busy in them, and every shade of sentiment, opinion, and belief gets into print and is read by all sorts of people. Each kind finds its own, as the magnet finds the particles of iron in the rubbish heap, and as mercury finds grains of gold. Each also finds more readers when its presence is made known, and the sphere of its attraction is enlarged by judicious mention. Thus the novelists of one nation can be made to appear more desirable than those of another by persistent presentation to the public; the writers of one section of a country may be given a large importance by a united endeavour on the part of the press; one school of literary artists may be constantly commended; methods may be enlarged upon, theories defended, and motives approved.   For instance, the naturalism, so called, of a French school of fiction may be adroitly explained and continually presented until it shall seem the most desirable thing in a modern novel. Again, the realism which photographs life and character may be lauded until many are persuaded that the art of the camera is better than the art of the brush.   Perhaps all that is requisite is a confederacy of criticism to upset the constitution of things in morals and good taste. The difficulty and the safety both lie in the impossibility of agreement among the doctors. The majority are on the side of decency and progression toward that which is best. The uplifting of general levels in literature during the last century is due in no small degree to the elevated tone of the best criticism, while the poorest, in several senses, has been a dead weight in this movement, but not much of a drawback.   It has been too light to be a hindrance.   It has not had on its side the forces which help the most, while against its success has been the coöperation of the powers of evil, which are always weakest in the long warfare and are a hindrance rather than a help.   Their temporary triumph is usually followed by reverses and defeat, as, on the contrary, retrograde movements in history are succeeded by renewed and rapid progression, and years of dearth by periods of great abundance.

Wise criticism will accordingly take thought as to the side on which it is best to array itself in the contest that is always going on between the upward and downward forces in literature. No higher motive than policy need be urged, if right instincts are lacking.   To be on the winning side is not the sublimest appeal, to be sure, but if that happens to be the right side also, then the two motives will weigh with all except the perversely contrary.   Even these have their use in keeping the majority from too much complacency and from letting their armour rust.

To address the critic's higher sense of the best that is thought and can be known is hardly needful.   Those who have it in other directions will see its value in litera- *The critic should know and commend the best literature.* ture, which, next to daily converse, is the strongest agency in making character.   What is good for people to read, especially for the young, the born critic, or the educated, knows as truly as the painter knows the colours on his palette, or whether a complexion is light or dark. The reader also may have some sense of the complexion of a book—after he has read it. He may know before, if a trustworthy critic has advertised its colour as dark or light; and it may be worth something to the reader to know which, especially if rumour and fame have heralded and accompanied the publishing. He may wish to know if a given book will be an angel in his house, or at least what kind of an angel. Will the messenger's charming or enthralling story leave a feeling of satisfaction or of discontent with the best features of the present order of things ? If of dissatisfaction, will it be of the nobler sort which looks towards higher ideals and their fulfilment ? These are some of the things which a busy man expects the highest criticism to tell him before he buys the book that everybody is said to be reading and takes it home for sons and daughters to read. Subtleness is considered as one of the essential features of narration and portrayal in this introspective age. Sometimes it is so subtle that one must think twice to catch the writer's real meaning. Such writing will need careful examination and faithful interpretation, and sometimes the placing of danger signals. This pioneer task, like the survey of unexplored sea-bottoms, demands skill and training.

Not every novice, not every well-meaning or right-minded reader can accomplish it for a community, whatever his own impressions may be. He must know something of the condition and sensibility of the public conscience, both moral and intellectual, and the character of much that is offered to it. Here, then, is the greatest responsibility of the critic, to know the beneficial and the adverse elements in the literary atmosphere. His senses must be keener than other men's, his knowledge wider and more certain. He should be able to scent contagion in balmy breezes, and discern wholesome influences in a storm. It should not be beyond him to note the larger movements of the seasons and the years with their tendencies and prophecies and fulfilments in letters. In all his work his ambition should be to win that confidence which compels attention and respect, and eventually establishes the authority to guide a constituency or a nation of readers to the best examples of the literature of knowledge and the literature of power.

XX

THE CRITIC'S AMBITIONS

"Talent is rare, vanity credulous, and glory seductive."
VILLEMAIN.

THERE is no good reason why a critic should not have his ambitions as well as other men. The main consideration is that they be clearly understood in their nature and limits. This, of course, depends upon the view each critic takes of his occupation, its methods, aims, and possibilities. If this view be fair and just, ambition will be to him what Sir Francis Bacon defined it to be, " like a humour that maketh men active, earnest, full of alacrity, and stirring." But so much depends upon the view. There has at times been a general impression that working critics as a class have not always had an exalted opinion of their vocation, that they have too commonly regarded it as a subordinate department in

Ambitions
shaped by
view of
his art.

literature and something which could be com-
mitted to apprentices. Someone has face-
tiously termed it " a department of letters
which, of course, requires no output but the
power to read and write." How far occasion
for such remark has been given in the actual
turning off of book notices and reviews must
be left to editors to conjecture. The best of
them doubtless have notions of what might be
done if there were nothing else to do in a newspaper office. The critic himself, however, is
at liberty to have his ideals, and to work toward
them amidst the pressure of various obligations,
as every other man must whose ambitions reach
beyond his daily task.

If the critic's ambitions are shaped by his
conceptions of the art, it would not be strange
to find these aspirations somewhat   *Therefore*
various in character. The one paral-   *various*
lel which is nearest is the diversity of   *ambitions.*
ambitions which are possible in the pursuit
of an education in a single university. Leaving out all differences which proceed from
different courses of study and aims in life,
the variety of college ambitions is something
remarkable; running from scholarly attainment
down through intellectual, athletic, and social
scales, which are themselves graded again.
Are there ten students who have the same

definite purpose in going to college, and who keep the same for four years ? Has the man who intended to read for the highest honours, and to take them, ever been known to take up finally with the championship in chess or whist ? Or has the prospective captain of the Nine or Eleven ever consoled himself for not winning that honour by becoming a squire of dames, forsaking the ball-field for the ball-room ? In a similar fashion there must be a diversity of ambitions in the arena of criticism, judging by achievements. One turns to art, another to the drama, another still to social affairs, a fourth to speakers from the pulpit and platform, a fifth to literature.   In this last class —the only one here contemplated—there would be as many more subdivisions if, in the present state of criticism, the kinds of work to be passed upon did not far outnumber the examiners. Accordingly it is next to impossible for such to become experts in any single direction, as in matters of science or history, philosophy or poetry. Consequently the qualities which are useful in all departments are most desirable, and will contribute most to the ambitions of the all-round critic.

In enumerating these it will be excusable to pass over the inferior ambitions. If anyone in these days cherishes aspirations toward mere sharpness, severity, and smartness he may be passed over as one born a century too late. If he assails those who differ from him in opinion, or those against whom he has a personal dislike or grudge, he belongs still farther back, say, in the carboniferous age of criticism. If he makes his personal likes and dislikes the ultimate test of good and bad, he should be ranked with mollusks, which do the same. But the clam has no ambitions, so far as known, and must be left to his instincts. Fortunately the primordial divisions in the animal and intellectual kingdom do not constitute the whole of it. Therefore it is permitted to turn from these and their tastes to higher orders and their higher aims. In observing these it will not be possible to keep out of mind the ideal critic, with exalted notions of his craft and superior standards of excellence.

Higher ambitions only are contemplated here.

It may not be fair to demand that he shall possess certain natural gifts which may have been denied him, such as keenness of perception and a judicial spirit. But if he have not these he need not attempt to be a critic. These gifts, and a few others, are nature's endowment, the lack of which can be but partially supplied by the sincerest endeavour. They will accordingly have to be

The ideal critic.

left out of the scope of attainable ambitions. These must be such as are within the reach of strenuous effort and honest purpose, and such as can be acquired.

Among the first of them is a true conception of the critic's mission, as distinguished from false, partial, or petty views of it. *His requisites.* Suppose that this be considered as "the promotion of good taste in letters,"—a general aim, but widely inclusive in its sweep. If this be kept steadily in mind it will be found to include many questions of methods and many working principles of practical criticism. Such a steadfast purpose will also help to solve some difficulties that are always springing up in the way. It will be one of the primary laws to which the bewildered critic may revert when conflicting interests and motives beset him.

The promotion of good taste involves first of all the possession of it, or a knowledge of what it is, by the critic himself. *Promotion of good taste in literature.* He is fortunate if this be inborn; but it may also be acquired. Study under guidance, and constant association with what is best in literature, and equally persistent renunciation of what is not best, will do much toward the cultivation of correct taste. Such observation and association is as effective in literature as in art. The cheap chromo and the cheaper print educate only the deficient in taste. They may be a step upward from nothing, but only the first step; necessary, perhaps, but not to the connoisseur. He cannot afford to risk harm to his keen sense of high art by giving them more than a passing glance. Nor can the guide in literature becloud his vision of what is worth most by dabbling in second- and third-rate productions. They have their downward educating power, just as effective for being unconscious. Everyone knows the contagious influence of dialects and provincialisms upon his speech. The New Englander soon "reckons" in Virginia, "allows" in Tennessee, and the stranger from Kentucky at length comes to "guess" in Massachusetts and five neighbouring States. In nothing more than in reading is a man known by the company he keeps, and the critic is known by his uncorrupted standard of good taste.

For charity's sake let this be supposed to be as good as Matthew Arnold deemed his own. How shall it be made promotive of the same in others ?—since the critic does not, of all men, live unto himself. On the contrary, he has a wide and varied clientèle looking to him for direction. Can he imbue them with the principles

involved in his own expression of his tastes ?
Not unless these conform to the best spirit of
the time.   As a general proposition to be defended successfully it would be much safer to
have said, " the ruling spirit of the time."
But suppose that should happen to have a
downward tendency, as it had at the time of
the Restoration, or as it may now be having in
things dramatic ?   It is easy to go with the
current, and not easy to stem it.   In these
circumstances the critic will see the advantage
of having constantly before him the cardinal
principle of his art, " the promotion of good
taste."   He may need to write it upon the
wall before him, and to bind it as a frontlet
between his eyes.   His business is to direct
the current and to help divert it if it is going
wrong.   He will do this best by emphasising
those books which approach nearest to the
standards of excellence that are recognised by
the best sentiment of the age.   This may not
mean by the loudest, or even the most widely
prevailing.   In these days, and in English-
speaking lands, such a spirit can be reckoned
on as a force out of all proportion to its numerical strength.   It holds the balance of power.
The burden of proof and of justification lies
with those who are not of it, but against it.
Therefore the critic can be sure of ultimate if

not immediate backing and support. To be a leader and a steadfast advocate in such a cause is an ambition worthy any writer. If the true power of great authors lies in " their utterance of ennobling and health-giving emotions,'' then the true function of critics lies in the added impulse and momentum they can impart to such work by timely and cordial endorsement and commendation. Something more than mere literary taste and something higher than good style are here contemplated; but they are by no means to be overlooked on account of an exalted ethical tone. Here is an opportunity for the critic's discrimination between a literary and a moral standard. When both are high, the best is accomplished. But the excellence of Burke need not be confounded with that of Bunyan, or compared with it, nor Poe's weird stories with Hawthorne's.

What warrant, however, is the director of public taste to have that the multitude, or even a respectable part, of his readers will accept and follow his suggestions ? This question does not affect his obligation to stand by his colours, and like personified wisdom to " call to the simple ones, How long will ye love simplicity ?'' The *noblesse oblige* of his position enforces his duty without consideration of results and successes. According to his ability, his ambition is to make the best in letters appear desirable in order that readers may find, sooner or later, that it is most desirable and satisfactory. He may have to do something more than give his word for it. Reasons will be asked for which he must be able to give. He must educate by pointing out, illustrating, and comparing; by analysis and exposition, by italics even, by anything which will make people see what they are likely to overlook or be insensible to in this hasty and somewhat book-hardened age. In so far as he does this, will his criticism be recognised as reasonable as distinguished from dogmatic. It will accordingly have the authority which judgment, founded upon published reasons, has over the unsupported dictum of personal opinion. It will have the advantage that the later criticism in this century has over that at the end of the last; that which the analytic and reasoned estimates of Lowell have over the fist-pounded verdicts of Doctor Samuel Johnson. The time has passed when people accepted unquestioningly the proclamation of self-constituted autocrats. '' Give us your reasons, and we will reserve the liberty to judge of their value,'' is an article in the declaration of independence by the republic of letters. Therefore the magistrate, the director, and even the humble guide in letters have more difficulty than the ancient magnate had who said, " This medicine is good for me; let everybody swallow it ": or, " This food is bad for the public because I was not brought up on it." Unless one can show that it is good or bad for the average man and in the nature of things, the multitude will reserve assent. Incidentally this doubles the labour of the critic, and sets the goal of a worthy ambition farther away. To show why his taste is in harmony with the best, and why the best should be followed, and that it is for the ultimate advantage and interest of the reader to follow it—to do this with even a moderate success, is one of the highest ambitions a critic can cherish who has right-minded views of his vocation.

If he accomplishes the last of these purposes, making the reading public read that which he has told them is best, he has in so far effected a reform which always needs to be carried on. It is something to maintain a successful struggle against downward tendencies in literary taste. It is something more to direct the restlessness and the eagerness of the active and the aspiring and the ambitious into helpful and healthful channels. Villemain truly said that " the love of letters, like other loves, blinds, misleads, and deludes, both with regard to ourselves and others: it mistakes the ardour of its aspirations for the measure of its strength: it is impatient of every obstacle, and often requires to be arrested in its progress." Here the useful offices of the good critic are needed to tell the reader what is worthy of his attention and devotion and what he can afford to pass by unnoticed. For in this time when five books of fiction are published daily—thirty thousand in the last eighty years, not to count an equal number in all other departments of literature taken together, and as many more of current periodicals—in this multiplication of pages and columns the one necessity of every reader is selection, and selection of the fittest. If this is the reader's necessity, it is the critic's duty. Not to provide a list of a hundred books, however excellent in themselves; for there might not be five that would be best for a hundred different persons, and these five they will be likely to find for themselves, or to have read already. Samuel Rogers, the poet, used to say, that when a new book came out he always took up an old one to read. In the flood of new books, which, like new citizens, are coming into our communities, there are the good and

the indifferent and the bad; and the critics are
the commissioners of examination, registration,
and appraisal. They are in this country the
last survival of a censorship of books which,
beginning with a suggestion as far back as
Plato, has found expression in the laws of almost every nation since. A censorship which
burnt the works of Protagoras and the sacred
writings of the early Church, came near sup-
pressing *Paradise Lost*, and peered over the
shoulders of authors and editors in all Europe
down to the middle of this century, exists here
and now only in the general sentiment of the
better part of the public, and in laws against
publications of a scandalously immoral character and against libel. Of this public, unwritten
sentiment the critic is the authorised spokesman, so far as there can be any authorisation.
He may be a non-commissioned officer, but he
has the chance to do more than yeoman service.
In his line there is no higher ambition, and the
road to promotion is always open. If his ambitions are for the prevalence of what is best in letters, and to sit as counsellor and judge, there is
always a vacant chair in this elective judiciary.
The patrician sentiment in literature will see to
it that Mugillanus the noble is chosen, until a
plebeian taste predominates and elects Rutilius,
a commoner. It is a part of the censor's obli-

gation to do his utmost to prevent such a decline in taste as will permit the domination of the rabble. When this duty becomes the ambition of all critics, there will be no anxiety about permanent tenure of office—unless some Marcus returns who, having held the censorship for two terms, gets a law passed against third-term occupancy by himself—and his successors. But that was in republican Rome; besides, his experience as estimator of moral, political, and literary values may not have been a fortunate one, like some of our own administrations.

There are always the highest literary ambitions, beckoning the critic on into fields of the Greater Criticism. He will recall names in the history of his art that have made it a " field of the cloth of gold " in literature itself, apart from its other achievements. It is not necessary to recount these names here, since most of them have already been mentioned, and selection might be invidious. To everyone will occur those of Lowell and Arnold and Sainte-Beuve as nearest in time and place, and as exemplars of their art whom it would be a great honour to approach. Such men lift the craft into the higher planes of thought and composition, and make carping censure, thoughtless strictures, and uninformed qualification unworthy of the

name of criticism. They belong among the
creators of literature, occupying a place as distinct and honourable as the poets and historians, the essayists and novelists, who have built
the fabric of English language and letters. The
man who shall find his name enrolled with theirs
by the electors of the future may account himself to have attained to one of the highest
literary ambitions. Yet somewhere in all lands
as good critics as they, have been and are
growing up, unrecognised, or beginning to be
observed, or possibly already taking their
places on the bench. If inquiry were made as
to their whereabouts, it might be replied, Read
the current literature of criticism, and apply to
editors and publishers for further information.
If the road by which they have come to distinction be a still more interesting subject of
inquiry, the critics themselves may be able to
answer some questions: but there will always be
some others which they cannot answer, except
in their own case,—secrets which every man
must discover for himself. If they are found
at all, it will be by diligent cultivation of that
measure of literary judgment one may happen
to possess. Even this may not be discovered
without some attempt to estimate, appreciate,
and build upon works which are worth such
attention. Once fairly begun, these processes

admit of indefinite expansion, leading the thoughtful and discriminating reader into wide fields and to the discovery of treasures hidden from the superficial and unobservant who are evermore hurrying on to find a region which shall yield its wealth to the passer-by without labour and without pains. It is no unworthy office to call such back continually to see what resources they are unmindful of, that riches are lying undeveloped all around them, and that Ophir is at their doors.

INDEX

A

I

J

R

WORKS IN LITERATURE

THE LITERARY HISTORY OF THE AMERICAN REVOLUTION.

By MOSES COIT TYLER, Professor of American History, Cornell University. Two volumes, sold separately. 8°, each $3.00

Volume I., 1763-1776; Volume II., 1776-1783.

" Prof. Tyler's newest work is rich, stimulating, informing, and delightful. And it is not only fascinating itself, but it is a luminous guide into the whole abundant, varied, and alluring field of our revolutionary literature: poetry, belles-lettres, biography, history, travel, and crackling controversy."—GEORGE W. CABLE in *Current Literature.*

A HISTORY OF AMERICAN LITERATURE DURING THE COLONIAL TIME.

By MOSES COIT TYLER. New edition, revised. Two volumes, sold separately. 8°, each $2.50

Volume I., 1607-1676; Volume II., 1676-1765.

Agawam edition. Two vols. in one, 8°, half leather . $3.00

THE LITERARY MOVEMENT IN FRANCE DURING THE NINETEENTH CENTURY.

By GEORGES PELLISSIER. Authorized English version, by ANNE G. BRINTON, together with a General Introduction. 8° $3.50

The eminent French critic M. Ferdinand Brunetière says of this: "M. Pellissier's work is no less the picture than the history of contemporary literature. In addition, it is also the philosophy of, or rather describes, the evolution of the literary movement of our country."

AMERICAN LITERATURE, 1607-1885.

By Prof. CHARLES F. RICHARDSON, of Dartmouth College. Two vols., 8°, pp. xx + 535,456 . . . . $6.00

Popular edition. Two vols. in one, half bound, 8°, pp. xx + 992 . . . . $3.50

Part I.—The Development of American Thought.

Part II.—American Poetry and Fiction.

" It is acute, intelligent, and original, showing true critical instinct and a high order of literary culture."—*Indianapolis Journal.*

G. P. PUTNAM'S SONS, NEW YORK AND LONDON.

ORATORY.

THE OCCASIONAL ADDRESS.

Its Literature and Composition ; A Study in Demonstrative Oratory. By Lorenzo Sears, L.H.D., Professor in Brown University, author of "A History of Oratory," etc. 12mo, $1.25

A HISTORY OF ORATORY AND ORATORS.

A Study of the Influence of Oratory on Politics and Literature, with Examples from the Lives of the Famous Orators of the World's History. By Henry Hardwicke, Member of the New York Bar, and Author of " The Art of Living Long and Happily," etc. 8° $3.00

AMERICAN ORATIONS.

From the Colonial Period to the Present Time, selected as specimens of eloquence, and with special reference to their value in throwing light upon the more important epochs and issues of American history. Edited, with introduction and notes, by the late Alexander Johnston, Professor of Jurisprudence in the College of New Jersey. Re-edited, with new material and historical notes, by James A. Woodburn, Professor of American History and Politics in Indiana University. In four series, each complete in itself, and sold separately. Large 12°, gilt top, per volume $1.25

BRITISH ORATIONS.

A selection of the more important and representative Political Addresses of the past two centuries. Edited, with introduction and notes, by Charles K. Adams. 3 vols., 16° $3.75
Half-calf, extra 7.50

GREAT WORDS FROM GREAT AMERICANS.

Comprising the Declaration of Independence ; the Constitution of the United States, with notes ; Washington's Circular-Letter of Congratulation and Advice to the Governors of the Thirteen States ; Washington's First and Second Inaugural Addresses and his Farewell Address ; and Lincoln's First and Second Inaugural Addresses and his Gettysburg Address. 18°, pp. 207 . . . 75 cts.
Citizens' edition. Illustrated. 12°, gilt top . . $1.50

G. P. PUTNAM'S SONS

NEW YORK AND LONDON